T0316411

Re-reading Economics in Literature

Re-reading Economics in Literature

A Capitalist Critical Perspective

Matt Spivey

LEXINGTON BOOKS
Lanham • Boulder • New York • London

Published by Lexington Books
An imprint of The Rowman & Littlefield Publishing Group, Inc.
4501 Forbes Boulevard, Suite 200, Lanham, Maryland 20706
www.rowman.com

6 Tinworth Street, London SE11 5AL, United Kingdom

British Library Cataloguing in Publication Information Available

Library of Congress Cataloging-in-Publication Data Available
Library of Congress Control Number: 2020944656

ISBN 978-1-7936-3447-4 (cloth)
ISBN 978-1-7936-3448-1 (electronic)

Contents

Introduction

I did not set out to defend Scrooge; it just turned out that way. Some years ago now, renowned economist and *New York Times* columnist Paul Krugman opened a pre-Christmas piece by comparing several Republican politicians to the infamous Ebenezer Scrooge of Charles Dickens's beloved novella, *A Christmas Carol*. I did not care whom he was mocking, as all politicians are deserving of it at one time or another. Rather, what bothered me about the article was that Krugman referenced a famous piece of literature—and got it wrong. What Krugman attempted to pull off was a sly editing maneuver of Dickens's original text in order to confirm his own ideological point. Krugman explained, like most of us have been taught, that Scrooge was unwilling to help the needy, as exemplified by his refusal to donate to two poverty relief workers who knock on his door on Christmas Eve. What Krugman, and most readers, ignore is the reason *why* Scrooge denies donating. Scrooge refuses to give because he knows of numerous government programs in place that were specifically implemented to battle poverty, that he openly discusses with the relief workers.

When asked to donate to the charity, Scrooge wonders if the prisons, workhouses, and the Poor Law system are still in place to house those who lack food and shelter. When the relief workers answer yes, Scrooge says, "Oh I was afraid, from what you said at first, that something had occurred to stop them in their useful course. I'm very glad to hear it." As the relief workers continue to plead for a donation, Scrooge clarifies his stance: "I help to support the establishments I have mentioned: they cost enough: and those who are badly off must go there" (Dickens 44–45). Scrooge, like the poor, has become reliant on government to solve social problems rather than the generosity of individuals. It is not Scrooge's meanness that keeps him from donating; it is that he assumes he doesn't need to because someone else (the government) will do it for him through the use of the very tax dollars he has already contributed. Scrooge is actually *defending* the welfare state. Scrooge's transformation by the end of the story is based not upon his suddenly becoming a swell guy who loves everyone and gladly gives his money away. Scrooge changes as a character because he realizes the power of the individual and the failures of government. He learns of the possibility that more might be accomplished to reduce poverty and promote happiness through individual initiative than by government coercion and inefficient

1

bureaucracies. *A Christmas Carol* can thus be read as a story of individual and capitalistic triumph and enlightenment, not the evils of industrialization that everyone has assumed. We have often only heard one side of the story—the anti-capitalist side, and its accompanying leftist, statist, collectivist, bureaucratic connotations—when it comes to integrating economic principles with important literature. Thus began my quest for a capitalist literary criticism.

Literary criticism, since its inception, has always progressed according to the method by which virtually all artistic endeavors have mutated, succeeded, and advanced. That is, by reacting to models, styles, and purposes that preceded it. Early approaches in formalism were challenged by the structuralist movement, which was eventually challenged by cultural studies critics in Marxism, feminism, post-colonialism, and others. And those avenues have since been taken to new heights through the development of minority studies, queer studies, eco-criticism, and more. It is entirely natural for the evolution of literary criticism to reflect the vast revisions and reinterpretations literature has undergone. As analyses of text, genre, and authorship gave way to a multifaceted foci on social, cultural, and economic influences, literary criticism became nearly synonymous with social activism. Feminist criticism began analyzing gender dynamics in an effort to subvert male dominance in literary production specifically and in cultural consciousness generally. Postcolonial criticism took on a similar mission by attempting to bring perspective and create voice for the imperialized and colonized peoples not only in the West, but throughout the world. In the economic realm, Marxist criticism sought to expose power relations among social classes, challenge the historical authority of the wealthy, and redefine cultural awareness as an oppressive product of hegemonic ideologies. It is this last form, anti-capitalist literary criticism, against which the evolution of literary analysis will react here. A new interpretation of economic study in literature has recently commenced, just as so many other criticisms developed. Rebellion against tradition, subversion of hegemony, and innovation in thought will define this emerging form just as it has for so many others. Anti-capitalist literary criticism may have attained the very quality it located in previous studies of literature: out of sync with contemporary economic theory. An alternative has begun to be proffered to reinvigorate the conversation of the intersection of literature and economics that has become somewhat tired. Capitalist literary criticism is this emerging method.

My journey toward this project began with a reawakening to economic philosophy through friends with careers in the business world, as well as through closely following the tumultuous economic conditions of recent years, both in America and around the world. While I have always been a proponent of free-market economic philosophy, I can honestly say I never exactly knew why, other than its affiliation with freedom, individualistic achievement, and low taxes. I was quickly made aware through early literary criticism courses that professors and critics were nearly unanimous in their overt condemnation of the capitalistic perspective, and that the very hegemony of thought they despised so deeply had actually taken root amongst themselves. Alternative voices are discouraged, professional positions are protected through tenure, and salaries are maximized as teaching loads diminish. The power of critics to protect themselves from market forces may lead many toward the misunderstandings, or even blatant inaccuracies, I discover in their interpretations of history and human action.

The field of literary studies had no capitalistic voice—that is, until I came across *Literature and the Economics of Liberty: Spontaneous Order in Culture*. I discovered this brilliant work by Paul Cantor and Stephen Cox right around the time of the Krugman article. And I was hooked. This was the first book to integrate literary criticism with a specifically pro-capitalist economic foundation, and it presents this capitalist perspective through the methodology of the Austrian School of economics. Its insight represented the tip of the iceberg for what can be accomplished by revisiting prominent works of literature and applying sound philosophical and economic methodology. The ever-present anti-capitalist ideology now had competition, and I have been on board ever since.

In the Woodmansee and Osteen collection of new economic criticisms, Jack Amariglio and David Ruccio note that some economists get concerned upon hearing literary critics attempt to analyze economics: "The trouble with most literary critics who claim to do economic criticism is that their understanding of economics too often ends with Marx." This is akin to an economics scholar attempting "to intervene in literary or cultural debate but her knowledge of that debate ended with Matthew Arnold." Amariglio and Ruccio, who actually reside on the left side of the economic/political spectrum, state that at conferences and in papers, many literary critics offer "an embarrassment of riches in the frequent 'misuses' of the terms and understanding of 'economics' by way of employing the vague terminology of 'late capitalism' or 'consumer society'"(382). However, Paul Cantor writes, "Marxist literary critics deserve at least this much credit: they have made a plausible and even a persuasive case for the relevance of economics to literature and literary activity. Economics is a central realm of human activity, and to the extent that literature attempts to deal with human life, it must inevitably come to terms with economic issues" (7). Thus, I have endeavored to build upon this reimagining of literary theory. That being said, the relentless economic disputes between anti-capitalist views and Austrian capitalism have been discussed more elaborately and more expertly in other places and will, therefore, not be fully reexamined here. This, ultimately, is a work of literary criticism, not economics. And just as works of anti-capitalist literary criticism do not delve into the minutiae of every accompanying anti-capitalist economic principle, this work will follow the same pattern regarding capitalist literary criticism. Similarly, histories of economic criticism have already been written in a variety of places, and while I will offer a brief evolution in chapter 1, because the aim of this project is to advance this burgeoning form of economic criticism initiated by excellent scholars who have preceded me, such repetition has been and hopefully will be avoided here.

A few of the specific flaws in traditional, anti-capitalist approaches that will be addressed include the misrepresentation of the very definition of capitalism as an economic term; the lack of respect and authority of the literary reader in the role of consumer; the dismissal of entrepreneurial spirit of authorship and creativity; and the disregard for subjective valuation, a primary tenet of Austrian economic theory, in favor of outmoded labor and use theories of value. Anti-capitalist critics will immediately and undoubtedly describe capitalist literary theory as being a product of ideology. I do not intend to dispute that claim. After all, everyone has a worldview that has been shaped by something outside of themselves. The difference is in the shaping. Anti-capitalist theory is developed through a collectivist perception of social structures; capitalist theory will be developed through praxeology and objective historical analysis. Anti-capitalist theory intends to change the world, while pursuing an idealistic vision; capitalist theory intends to explain the world, while understanding its inherent limitations in doing so. Anti-capitalist theory was developed as a form of rebellion against those in power; capitalist theory will do precisely the same.

The vast majority of authors, critics, and professors of literature attend an anti-capitalist perspective regarding economic literary criticism. The same people that once claimed to struggle against hegemonic oppressors have actually become a version of Antonio Gramsci's hegemony. (Allow me to briefly share an anecdote of this in action. When I was in graduate school at a public university, Marx's *Communist Manifesto* appeared on reading lists for multiple literary criticism courses. However, the few times I attempted to interject Friedrich Hayek's work into class discussions, fellow students and professors looked at me as if I had begun speaking Klingon. Despite being a Nobel Prize winner and one of the leading intellectuals of the twentieth century, Hayek was entirely unfamiliar, while Marx was expected to be common knowledge.) It is now those that believe in individual liberty, inalienable rights, free enterprise, and rule of law that are the voiceless minority in literary arenas. Literary analysis as social commentary and political perspective has existed for many decades, and introducing this form of criticism is not intended to immediately create capitalists out of all theorists. However, the attempt must be made to shed a new and revealing light on literary studies that will expose long-held theories as incomplete at best and destructive at worst, and promote a flourishing era of individualism and entrepreneurship in literature. Good art has always been based upon freedom of expression and has often clashed with its surrounding culture. This path of economic literary criticism will be no different.

This analysis, when undertaken as individuals, ultimately leads to improvement in the literary criticism community as a whole. It is important for critics to forge new paths and explore them as individuals. By continuing the tired methodology of anti-capitalist forms of literary criticism, we have the potential to diminish the effectiveness of our goals. New voices and new perspectives are needed in order to move our field forward, seeking the best available criticisms and producing the most effective methods of literary analysis. Our profession depends upon the creativity of the individual; let us strengthen that foundation by embracing an alternative economic criticism. If we do, to the delight of anti-capitalist critics, our community will be better for it.

This book will explain some of the fundamentals of this form of economic literary criticism, one founded in capitalistic methodology, and how this model may be applied to the literature itself. In this project, I will offer extended economic readings of the following texts: Frederick Douglass's *Narrative of the Life of Frederick Douglass, an American Slave, Written by Himself* (1845), F. Scott Fitzgerald's *The Great Gatsby* (1925), John Steinbeck's *The Grapes of Wrath* (1939), Richard Wright's *Native Son* (1940), and Kurt Vonnegut's *Player Piano* (1952). I have chosen these particular works to highlight for three main reasons. First, they are distinctly "American." By that, I mean they are indicative of American economic themes that have existed since our founding: the power of the individual; the continuous negotiation between private and public interests; the role of government; economic mobilization; the influence of gender, race, country of origin, or other cultural factors on the economic process; the evolution of technology and industry; and other features that demonstrate economic relationships that have traditionally defined our nation and, thus, our creative projects like literature. Second, I focus on these texts for their timeliness in relation to major economic movements in America. Obviously, the institution of slavery during the mid–1800s was an important and controversial economic period in our nation, as was the interwar period that also included the Great Depression between the 1920s and 1940s, as was the post–war industrialization of the country during the 1950s. These latter decades saw the boom-and-bust cycle in full effect and witnessed the migration of millions of Americans from Midwest to West and from South to North in search of economic opportunity amid an explosion of innovation and production. And during each of these time periods, the conflict between individual freedom and government legislation was front and center in American political and economic life. Third, I have also chosen these texts and authors for their ubiquitous nature in the world of academics. Their prominence is exactly why they need reexamination from a new angle. The opportunity to assist college and high school students in rediscovering classic American texts by developing new interpretations should be one of the primary aims of the literary critic and teacher. Each of these texts, and many others like them, provide the wonderful juxtaposition of artistry and history, impassioned perspective and economic principles.

Chapter 1 of this book will begin by providing a brief historical framework for economic analysis of literature. While anti-capitalist literary criticism has morphed over the years, in order to accommodate its varying philosophical interpretations, historical inconsistencies, and tenuous relationship to the world outside of literary studies, it remains the generally prescribed method for analyzing literature from an economic perspective. While an anti-capitalist perspective does not always focus on specifically economic conditions, preferring often to highlight more abstract notions of interpretation, it still relies at its core on a perceived separation among classes, and by its extension in cultural studies, races and genders. Challenging the dynamics of power and subverting the evolutionary process of capitalism remain in the prevailing definition of anti-capitalist approaches, and as these themes are presented in literary contexts, literary studies have never experienced a truly alternative economic understanding of text. I will briefly summarize the movements of anti-capitalist literary criticism in order to demonstrate how a capitalist literary criticism will be placed historically and philosophically according to other junctions of economics and literature.

Once a contextual background of the anti-capitalist trends has been explicated, I will then challenge several of the primary tenets that define this prevailing criticism. Exposing some of the epistemological and methodological flaws in anti-capitalist literary criticism is a necessary component for offering a replacement form of criticism that is more consistently logical, consciously accessible, and conceptually workable. Capitalist literary criticism will seek to amend the flaws in economic interpretation that anti-capitalist approaches provide by demonstrating both the philosophical and practical advantages for endeavoring upon a new track of literary theory. Anti-capitalist criticism has retained its dominance in the literary arena for the simple fact that no alternative has been offered. These chapters aim to shift that paradigm.

Chapter 2 will focus on the most fundamental principle in economics: human capital. Every person in society, and every character in literature, can do something, be somebody. And beginning from the axiomatic principle that "humans act," we must begin with analyzing literature from the most basic element of economics: the individual. In this chapter, I will demonstrate how individuals, utilizing their own human capital (intelligence, effort, creativity, wit, and other personal attributes) improve their lives over the course of respective narratives, contrary to what anti-capitalist principles of class consciousness or hegemonic oppression traditionally offer in literary criticism. Frederick Douglass's esteemed autobiography, *Narrative of the Life*, will provide ample evidence of the power of individualism and the development of human capital, the most fundamental requisite for participation in the capitalist system. Facing incredible oppression based on race and class, Douglass overcame horrific obstacles to become an independent agent of human action and vital participant in free market capitalism. It is through his own words and voice that the presentation of a capitalist system based upon individual action will offer insight into the power of human capital as the basis for economic activity and the path to capitalistic achievement.

Chapter 3 will move from the laboring individual to the individual as part of society. Using F. Scott Fitzgerald's classic, *The Great Gatsby*, as the primary focus of this section, I will discuss a variety of economic principles that challenge much of the prevailing thought on Fitzgerald's masterwork. Deficit spending, debt, illegal bootlegging, "new money," commodification, and other economic concepts abound in this 1925 novel, and they deserve reconsideration. Also, I will create a metaphorical reading of the text's character relationships as a point of comparison with the Austrian business cycle. While the prevailing view of the work in literary criticism is harsh toward the lavish lifestyle of the *nouveau riche* and the frivolity of East Coast classifications of the American Dream, there is much more to be learned from the Austrian economic perspective of this work. Reinterpreting Gatsby's misguided goals, as well as his interactions as an economic agent, will be the predominant aim of this chapter.

Chapter 4 will leave the economic boom of Fitzgerald's 1920s and head toward the economic depression of John Steinbeck's 1930s. In his many works, Steinbeck is the voice for the common people, depicting farmers and laborers with a romantic quality that borders on mythological, if he weren't desperate to be so realistic. In many economic interpretations of his works, we are shown the greed of bankers, the harshness of employers, and the continuous obstacles that deter innocent workers from capitalistic success. However, what is rarely described in his most acclaimed work, *The Grapes of Wrath*, is the distorted outlook of the novel's author and its characters' injurious economic beliefs. Steinbeck and his characters suffer from unfamiliarity of agricultural market forces, unwillingness to adjust to alternative opportunities, and naïve optimism in federal government that led to devastating interventions that increased the plight of laborers and prolonged the horrific conditions of the economic depression. Steinbeck effectively leads us to feel sympathy for the Joad family, but we are never exposed to the economic circumstances that truly damaged families, farmers, and workers in the 1930s and exist even to this day. I aim to bring to light those economic principles that have been lost in decades of traditional literary criticism.

Chapter 5 will move from the rural life of Steinbeck to the city of Richard Wright. Richard Wright's *Native Son* will offer endless opportunities for dissecting urban economics of 1940, as race and class combine in the city of Chicago. Protagonist Bigger Thomas feels like many early twentieth century African-Americans — trapped in social structures and belittled by authorities — who attempted to understand identity and place amid oppression of various kinds. But I argue that Bigger's perception of reality is not always congruent with history, and the majority of perceived injustices he encounters are actually rationally explained through economic reasoning. Capitalist criticism offers an entirely new way of reading this novel and of understanding the historical, cultural, and social conditions Bigger Thomas inhabits.

Chapter 6, the final segment of this book, will bring us to the post–World War II industrialization and middle class expansion of the 1950s with an in-depth study of Kurt Vonnegut's *Player Piano*. In this text, the role of mechanization in cultural development and the loss of individualism in the face of corporate bureaucracies provide a wealth of opportunities for examining the economics of industry. Vonnegut's dystopian presentation of capitalistic overreach will be supplemented from a standpoint of both technological expansion, as well as the provision of opportunity and well-being across social strata. I intend to discuss Vonnegut's message of labor using historical evidence from both the nineteenth and twentieth centuries, as well as more contemporary economic theory. In addition to providing a logical conclusion to an examination of tumultuous economic changes ranging from the mid–1800s through the first half of the 1900s, this chapter reexamines key themes that have emerged throughout previous chapters, such as individualism, government intervention, and business activity.

I will then conclude the book by revisiting the path we will have traveled, from anti-capitalist criticism to Austrian economic criticism. I will remind the reader of the primary premise that this project seeks to define: a capitalist literary criticism, rooted in Austrian economic principles, may be more congruent with literary analysis and production than an anti-capitalist perspective, and its implementation in the academy and the critical marketplace has the potential to improve not only literary studies, but our understanding and influence on the real world around us. We navigate this world as individuals, making millions of specific decisions based on millions of pieces of specific information available only to us as individuals. And we approach literature as individuals. Our lives are not predetermined by class or any other social construct; our analysis of literature should be no different. An Austrian economic approach to literature is commensurate with the way we live our lives — attempting to discern the continuous cause and effect relationships that define the paths of life.

ONE

The Austrian School of Economic Literary Criticism

In order to understand the development of a new branch of literary theory, as well as to legitimize it and to test its accuracy and usefulness, we must first understand its philosophical origins. The premise from which the theory discussed in this book begins lies with humanity's ability to reason. Austrian economist Ludwig von Mises explains, "Reason is man's particular and characteristic feature." It is perhaps the most vital component of our personhood, as our high neurological level of reasoning appears to be distinctly human, and it guides every single thought and action we take. Reason, subsequently, causes action. "Man alone has the faculty of transforming sensuous stimuli into observation and experience," Mises writes. "And man alone can arrange his various observations and experiences into a coherent system." This does not mean that reasoning necessarily leads to an understanding of an all-encompassing and eternal truth. It simply means that thinking is directly correlated to acting; and some degree of thinking, conscious or unconscious, always comes first. To mentally consider an action to be taken later, and then to mentally ruminate on an action previously taken, is a uniquely human quality and clearly demonstrates that an inherent and indissoluble bond exists between thought and action. It is through reasoning that humans create cause and effect relationships. And if a cause and effect relationship guides human action, a theory can describe this. Mises writes, "Action without thinking, practice without theory are unimaginable." Consider, however, that the thinking process may prove to be illogical, the resulting action unworkable, and the theory unverifiable; this does not necessarily negate that thinking and action and this theory about them are inextricably linked. All theory is assumed to be correct by the thinker

9

and its premise able to be demonstrated through action (*Human Action* 187).

In practice, these relationships between thinking, action, and theory are easy to identify. The emergence of a less mundane and more philosophical theory, such as a literary theory, is no different. Up to this point, Marxist literary theory has been the prevailing perspective in combining the study of economics with the study of literature. Though Marxist theory has undergone numerous iterations to accommodate various logical problems, at its root, it follows a generally anti-capitalist methodology. In the Marxist paradigm, subjects must first think about how to survive in their political and economic circumstance before they can pursue anything of culture, which includes art and literature. Thus, in order to participate and take action in culture, humans must acquiesce to the political and economic power structure in which they reside. It is in this state, many Marxists would contend, that the relationships between base and superstructure reify, ideologies emerge, and hegemonies prevail. Therefore, any cultural product that humans produce is a direct result of the basic political and economic circumstances. Though this is a simplified version of the foundational premise of Marxism, we can see how this theory can be utilized for understanding the complexities of art and literature. However, it is in the testing where theory must prove its validity. Mises writes, "Fiction is a favored vehicle for this kind of [anti-capitalist] procedure, as there is little fear that anyone will try to refute its assertions in detail by logical criticism. It is not the custom to inquire into the accuracy of particular remarks in novels and plays" (*Socialism* 465). I believe what is provided here and in the following chapters is an alternative way of providing a coherent economic literary theory, while also improving its amenability for confirmation and application.

Economic criticism implies any form of literary criticism in which economic principles are addressed and elucidated in literature and, additionally, it seeks a correlation of economic processes with the creation, dissemination, and reception of literature. But within this focus of examination, a wide range of analyses may take place. The use of basic economic concepts, such as money, debt, and trade, may be explored in literature. Production of literature and the commodification of art, homologies of representation and exchange, as well as more complicated studies, such as narratology and linguistics, all fall under the purview of economic criticism. But until only recently, proffering an economic reading of literature has almost always been synonymous with an anti-capitalist reading of literature. Therefore, an alternative view must accomplish more than simply providing a diametrically disparate position, one which could be interpreted as an aggressive fluctuation from one end of the economic spectrum to the other purely for the sake of opposition. A pro-market perspective on literature must indicate not only a divergence from anti-capitalist analyses, but an important supplement to and even an improvement upon the existing economic reading, demonstrating, ideally, that capitalism is more applicable to literary study and provides a greater capacity for discovery than traditional views. In order to examine an innovative form of criticism, however, we must first understand the process that has led us to this point and prepare ourselves for acknowledging the relationships between the past methodologies and those that are to follow.

During his time as a professor at University of Edinburgh, Adam Smith taught on history, politics, economics, morality, and philosophy, as we would expect. Many of these ideas he lectured on, of course, became published as his most famous texts, *The Theory of Moral Sentiments* (1759) and *The Wealth of Nations* (1776). But he also led lectures on language and literature. Smith's *Lectures on Rhetoric and Belles Lettres* demonstrate the historical tradition of a free-market thinker (which would only later be termed a "capitalist") attempting to engage with and improve upon the contemporary methodology of literary criticism. Smith approached the arts with a classical eye, privileging authorship and stylistic tradition, and he reverently nods to Platonism. Smith describes that while humans are self-interested beings, as he explains most famously in *The Wealth of Nations*, we maintain a sympathetic nature that is intently expressed in the arts, a theme which is elucidated even further in *The Theory of Moral Sentiments*. This sympathy is accomplished through mimesis, in which the literary reflects imaginative possibilities. Thus, it is in the act of imitation, and by being a spectator in such endeavors of imitation, whereby humans may then admire or criticize based on the concurrent development of taste or fashion. J. C. Bryce notes in his introduction to *Lectures on Rhetoric and Belles Lettres* that Smith took a comparative approach to literary criticism, or "the pin-pointing of an author's essential quality by putting his work alongside that of a practitioner in the same field or a kindred one" (qtd. in Smith 31). This technique of criticism did not please poet William Wordsworth, as he vehemently condemned Smith's lack of Romantic appreciation for literary beauty, calling him "the worst critic" Scotland had produced (qtd. in Smith 31–32). Though we may no longer remember Adam Smith for his contributions to literary thought, to be recognized by Wordsworth in such a public and combative display is evidence of Smith's influence on the arts during the late eighteenth century. Just as importantly, Smith's opinions on the arts greatly influenced his encompassing philosophy as exhibited by his later, more renowned, works.

Though Smith was an economist and a literary critic, it would be a stretch to label his form of criticism as economic. It would be two hundred years before Marc Shell's *The Economy of Literature* (1978) and Kurt Heinzelman's *The Economics of the Imagination* (1980) became two of the first texts to clearly define a purposeful movement toward a specifically economic literary criticism, since for Marx and Engels, neither literature

nor criticism was ever a strong focus. Various forms of integrating economic concepts into literary criticism, though, have existed since the first
half of the twentieth century. Walter Fuller Taylor's *The Economic Novel in
America* (1942) and Claude Flory's *Economic Criticism in American Fiction,
1792-1900* (1936) are useful sources for examining early cases of literary
and economic thought, specifically for American literature. By contrast,
the economic criticism I am outlining here has ventured beyond merely
recognizing economic conditions within literature, and instead has focused more thoroughly on the methodology and philosophy by which
we engage economics when we read literary works.

Martha Woodmansee and Mark Osteen's *The New Economic Criticism:
Studies at the Intersection of Literature and Economics* provides an extensive
history of the field and examines current trajectories regarding the interdisciplinary nature of economic literary study. However, even this infor-
mative collection of criticism, which does offer an interesting assortment
of texts and analyses, still largely reflects the traditionally dominant anti-
capitalist, collectivist, or leftist approach to literature. Though a few authors in the collection do question some of the practices of anti-capitalist
criticism, virtually none could be considered pro-capitalist. Economic literary criticism has morphed through versions of formalistic, psychoana-
lytical, post-structural, and historicist practices, but what remains consistent is the anti-capitalist philosophy buttressing or underpinning nearly
all of them. Paul Cantor humorously describes the traditional, and still
prevailing, formula for economic literary criticism: "mix quasi-Marxism
with vanguard Marxism, and add just a soupçon of fashionable French
thought (structuralist or poststructuralist) to give it flavor" (2). Challenging the long-standing heritage of anti-capitalist-infused literary study is a
daunting task, especially when the attempt to offer an alternative and
equally enlightening form of economic criticism has only recently come
to the literary critical realm.

Though Karl Marx never truly ventured into the realm of literary
theory, his ideas were carried forth in the works of literary critics through
numerous variations, while remaining stalwartly leftist in their foundations. György Lukács in the 1930s employed a revisionist version of
Marxism to examine the modern bourgeoisie by aiming at depictions of
reality, as he perceived it, in literature. In his influential 1938 essay "Real-
ism in the Balance," he describes his disdain for the Modernist literary
movement as being too subjective and personally removed from the realities of life that art is supposed to represent. Lukács's view of reality is
one in which capitalism is a "totality," a pervasive influence on every
way in which societies are constructed. This line of thinking is what
eventually propelled the anti-capitalist literary tradition forward. Mean-
while, as New Criticism became fashionable several decades later, economics as a social science became largely divorced from the literary text.
Economic criticism purposefully strayed from complicated authorial,

theoretical, or political implications in literature, focusing instead on economic terminology and tropes. This technique, however, limits the value of economic criticism, I believe, by constricting economics into closed, textual structures.

Through the dramatic cultural changes of the 1960s, 1970s, and 1980s, Marxist economic criticisms reemerged, and were greatly influenced by theorists outside of the literary arena, such as philosophers and sociologists. Theodor Adorno's arguments regarding aesthetics and the "culture industry" linked revised Marxist principles with artistic endeavors. Adorno believed that the mass production of art, particularly in the emerging media of the twentieth century (radio, film, television, etc.), simply reproduced homogenous and monopolistic ideas to be imbibed by foolish and passive consumers. Louis Althusser extended Marxist thought by borrowing from the philosophy of Antonio Gramsci and combining it with psychoanalysis to examine the conceptualization of ideology—most prominently in his renowned essay, "Ideology and Ideological State Apparatuses"—and the concept of ideology remains influential in literary, cultural, and political circles today. Raymond Williams examined the role of productive forces in shaping literature, ideology, and the reading class. This eventually led him to become a prominent voice in the emergence of the field of cultural studies, an offshoot of Marxist methodologies, with some of his most interesting work coming in *Culture and Society* (1958) and *Keywords* (1976), where he explores the effects of social and economic circumstances on language and even individual words themselves.

Literary critic Terry Eagleton ultimately clarified the Marxist vision in *Marxism and Literary Criticism* by defining Marxist criticism as a fundamental form of revealing, investigating, and comprehending ideologies, which include "the ideas, values, and feelings by which men experience their societies at various times. And certain of those ideas, values, and feelings are available to us only in literature. To understand ideologies is to understand both past and present more deeply; and such understanding contributes to our liberation" (viii). In recent decades, Fredric Jameson's critique of culture trends and capitalism's relationship to postmodernism have elevated Marxist (or "post-Marxist") literary thought to its current state. Obviously, numerous other, less-renowned critics have helped shape anti-capitalist economic criticism, but these continue to be a few of the standard-bearers. Economic literary criticism is so saturated with anti-capitalist influence that despite the wide range of popular and viable economic philosophies throughout history, anti-capitalism is largely the only economic approach present in literary studies. And while not every critic is necessarily anti-capitalist, somehow almost every economic literary criticism is.

A decidedly pro-market or capitalist form of new economic criticism is, however, starting to take shape. Key thinkers in the field today are still few and far between, as a free-market perspective of literature is only in its infancy. Perhaps the leading voices in this new form of economic literary criticism are Paul Cantor and Stephen Cox. Their recent text, *Literature and the Economics of Liberty*, is groundbreaking in its presentation of literary history and theory from an Austrian economic foundation, which could be more casually defined as libertarian or pro-capitalist; the Austrian School will be discussed at length in this project. In this volume Cantor and Cox offer an initial justification for an alternative to anti-capitalist literary criticism, as well as a variety of case studies for analyzing literature and its authors according to this new paradigm.

A few other studies have also begun to set out other new-economic themes that might be further explored in this nascent field. Allen Mendenhall deftly blends capitalism with political philosophy in his literary analyses in *Literature and Liberty*. And Edward Younkins dives deeply into specific business practices from a capitalist point of view in his expansive collection, *Capitalism and Commerce in Imaginative Literature*. Russell Berman, in *Fiction Sets You Free*, presents a study of literary autonomy, or creative individualism, throughout history, arguing for the positive relationship between free-market capitalism and the arts. He states that literature, at its core, is an exercise in imagination and liberty that can only achieve greatness and longevity via a system that allows for such free enterprise. In a more focused and traditional vein, Frederick Turner's *Shakespeare's Twenty-First Century Economics* demonstrates how language, ethics, and economics are intertwined in Shakespeare's works, producing a justification for free-market principles in which all humans can participate.

Other authors have begun to promote economic literary criticism by reaching out to both economists and literary critics. The work of Michael Watts, in a number of critical articles and particularly in his *The Literary Book of Economics*, provides dozens of textual examples to be employed by both literary scholars seeking economic components and economics scholars seeking literary representations. The interdisciplinary nature of this form of criticism is one of its most useful and practical qualities. Like Watts, other authors, such as Sharon O'Dair, Paul Delaney, and Lee Erickson do not necessarily present an overtly pro-capitalist perspective in each of their writings, but they make at least an attempt at recognizing some of the positives of presenting an alternative to anti-capitalist criticism. Many have published material in interdisciplinary forms where economics and literature are treated on equal footing, and some, such as Cantor and Delaney, actually have backgrounds in economic policy and philosophy. Thus, the field of critics standing in opposition to anti-capitalist literary criticism and forging a new economic criticism founded in capitalism is narrow, yet well-equipped and gaining ground. Anti-capitalist thinking, however, still dominates the economic literary discussions. And perhaps it is the very word *capitalism* that is the starting point for understanding where a new path might lead us.

The term *capitalist*, meaning simply one who owns capital, has existed for centuries. However, it was not Adam Smith, whom many consider to be the grandfather of free-market economic thought, who was responsible for instituting the term. Smith, in his most famous work, *The Wealth of Nations*, did not even use the word capitalist. Rather, he described his view of economics as simply, "Give me that which I want, and you shall have this which you want" (422). For Smith, and capitalists, human commerce results in a positive-sum exchange, whereby *both* the buyer and seller benefit. If they did not, they would not engage in trade in the first place. Therefore, through the voluntary exchange system of capitalism, everyone gains, reaching a mutually advantageous economy (DiLorenzo 2). Perhaps surprisingly, it was Karl Marx himself who coined the usage of *capitalist* in reference to the *economic system* of capitalism. The term is used over 2,600 times in his magnum opus *Das Kapital*, regularly as a pejorative, often a condemnation of the bourgeoisie and its perceived exploitation of the labor class.

At nearly the same time Marx was developing his theories of classical economics, Austrian law student and journalist Carl Menger, during his research into the discrepancies between classical theories and real world economic actions, began developing a new perspective that would soon culminate in the publication of his influential treatise, *Principles of Economics* (1871), just four years after the publication of the first segment of Marx's *Das Kapital*. This signaled the birth of the Austrian School, a branch of economic study that is still prominent today. Just as Austrian economics presented a challenge to the classical economics of Marx, England's David Ricardo, and even Adam Smith, it is this perspective and its defining methodology that will aid in contesting the prevailing economic influence in literary study today. For decades now, literary critics have attempted to show how economics exerts an influence on literature. But until only recently, that influence has come distinctly and solely from the anti-capitalist position. This project will incorporate into literary study a perspective of economics, and specifically of capitalism, based on the Austrian School. The Austrian vision of capitalism is perhaps not what the general public thinks it to be, and it is certainly not what traditional academics in most English departments think it to be.

Following Menger's lead, the Austrian School became fully developed under the philosophy of Ludwig von Mises, who is today considered the father of modern Austrian economic thought. In his groundbreaking works *The Theory of Money and Credit* (1912), *Socialism: An Economic and Sociological Analysis* (1922), *Liberalismus* (1927), and his behemoth defining text *Human Action* (1949), which will be cited heavily in this project for its immense depth and thorough explanation of the Austrian perspective, Mises clarified for a world audience a view of economics that was based not upon mathematical formulae to measure and predict human behavior, but rather on the logical deductions and axiomatic explications of human behavior itself. Mises's primary economic theory, that humans act purposefully in order to attain ends, defies the macroeconomic view of an underlying organization to economic activity, and instead posits that a spontaneous order (an elaboration on Smith's "invisible hand" description from the eighteenth century, and a precursor to a more detailed explanation later offered by Nobel laureate and Mises's former student, Friedrich Hayek) will emerge in economic interactions, whereby free people making free decisions are likely to arrive at efficient and effective market results.

The Austrian presentation of capitalism is simply one person willingly exchanging with another, without threat of coercion or force from each other or from government influence, each satisfying the other's transactional demand. It is this theory of capitalism that was misunderstood by Karl Marx in the mid–1800s and remains misrepresented by economists—and for our purposes here, literary critics delving into economics—to this day. What many critics of capitalism, particularly in the literary studies, fail to grasp is the defining economic perspective on key concepts like "exchange." In the anti-capitalist economic paradigm, mutually beneficial exchange, as defined by the Austrian School of capitalist thought, does not exist. The power relations that define anti-capitalist models ordain a zero-sum model, whereby profit and losses coexist simultaneously as one person (or business, or nation, etc.) benefits *at the expense* of another. Therefore, the market functions just as a state authority would, protecting one class while exploiting another, while continuously aiming to reproduce this dynamic. This zero-sum doctrine stands in direct contradiction to classical liberalism and Austrian economics because, according to the Austrian School, market interactions are *voluntary*; therefore, power dynamics do not inhere within exchange, and every individual is free to engage in market activity with every other individual in a positive-sum relationship. What proponents of anti-capitalism in both economics and in literary theory are actually criticizing is *mercantilism*. And if anti-capitalists more clearly understood their terminology, they would see that Austrians agree with the evils of mercantilism. In fact, Marx's disdain for such a system actually echoes Adam Smith's *Wealth of Nations*, which is largely a systematic repudiation of mercantilism.

Mercantilism blurs the line between private economic activity and coerced economic activity, and is usually sponsored by a state government for the purposes of protecting a particular ruling class. Since the anti-capitalist does not distinguish between authorities (there is simply the exploiters and the oppressed), that person will assume that the state and the market are one and the same, performing the same social function. For a true Austrian capitalist, however, the free market *cannot exist* when interfered with by a coercive government, for it undermines the vital foundation of voluntary interaction. Thus, according to the anti-capitalist, a capitalist is just another agent of the state, a force for exploitation, rather than a free person seeking unencumbered trade with other free persons. While hiding under a cloak of perceived capitalism, mercantilism is not indicative of free-market exchange at all. Due to the anti-capitalist's definition of terms, the critic has misnamed and misrepresented the opponent, not simply for being unable to see the difference, but because "the Marxist paradigm quite literally renders him *incapable* of making such a distinction" (Osterfeld 110). After all, if a Marxist begins to see the distinguishing factors of voluntary exchange, and recognize that the alternative (socialism, perhaps) is in fact the paradigm that promulgates power relations, the Marxist's understanding of economic action, and its accompanying worldview, may begin to crumble.

Other terms that often get misconstrued under the anti-capitalist definition of capitalism, when in fact they are not related to the free-market delineation of the term, include state capitalism, corporate capitalism (or crony capitalism), or any other form of mixed economy in which interventionism and government planning play an integral role in market interactions. The United States largely operates under a version of social market economy, whereby markets are nominally left free, except for particular regulatory measures and social programs, such as social security, welfare benefits, and the like. The Austrian School largely rejects all of these models, including the current U.S. form, for being overly interventionist. We must remember that capitalism according to the foundations of Austrian economics emphasizes the individual agent as a voluntary actor in an economic system in which a government's *sole provision* is to maintain laws that prevent deceit and coercion. "The state creates and preserves the environment in which the market economy can safely operate," Mises writes. "It protects the individual's life, health, and property against violent or fraudulent aggression" (*Human Action* 258). Any further involvement is antithetical to a true free-market economy. Obviously, as with anti-capitalist philosophies, there are gradations of this belief system (as even one of the heroes of Austrian economics, Hayek, believed in a very minimal social relief system), but the foundational principles, particularly those laid out by Mises, will be highlighted here.

Mises explains that confusing the terminology of capitalism, or relabeling it according to a protectionist time period by identifying "late capitalism—as the Marxians call it" only attempts to conflate concepts that remain fundamentally different:

> The concept of capitalism is as an economic concept immutable; if it means anything, it means market economy. One deprives oneself of the semantic tools to deal adequately with the problems of contemporary history and economic policies if one acquiesces in a different terminolo-

gy. This faulty nomenclature becomes understandable only if we realize that the pseudo-economists . . . who apply it want to prevent people
from knowing what the market economy really is. (*Human Action*
269–70)

Osterfeld adds that misunderstandings over terms may obstruct important opportunities for discourse:

> The inability of the Marxist paradigm to distinguish between capital-
> ism and mercantilism has resulted in an unfortunate terminological
> confusion which has meant that classical liberals and Marxists have
> often talked past one another when they were, in fact, in substantial
> agreement, at least on certain key issues regarding the state, such as its
> role in generating class conflict and turning trade into a situation in
> which one group benefits at the expense of another. (111–12)

In order to fully comprehend what a capitalist form of literary criticism
looks like, we must be clear on our terminology of capitalism itself. I
contend that anti-capitalists have usually erred in this understanding,
and therefore, any attempt to dialogue about literature from an economic
perspective must begin with a clarification of this fundamental point. The
capitalism represented here in this project is entirely from an Austrian
economic point of view, and each of the following chapters, along with
the corresponding textual analyses, will maintain this position.

The Austrian School offers further credibility as an original approach
to economics and literary studies, as it is not reliant upon any religious
affiliation or political party for promoting or defending its rationale.
Many Austrian economists are agnostics or atheists because of their beliefs in humanism and evolution, as indicated by their support in economics of praxeology (the study of human action) and spontaneous order
(the automatic emergence of market and other social efficiencies). Many
are also unaligned with particular political organizations, largely due to
the failures of both major American parties to adhere to the principled
economic approaches offered by the Austrian School. I will pursue such
nonpartisan critique in both chapter 3 and chapter 4, as I discuss the
disastrous effects of both Republican and Democratic policies during certain points in our nation's economic history. Thus, due to its spirit of
independent thought and individualistic action, the Austrian defense of
capitalism is less ideological than other economic perspectives, even
among those who appear to represent similar positive interpretations of
capitalism. As a result, I will strive to write in such a way so that at no
point in this analytical work will a particular political ideology emerge.
The same cannot be said for various anti-capitalist criticisms.

The aim of this project is to recognize the positive connection between
the Austrian School of economic philosophy and the field of humanities
in general and literary studies in particular. Esteemed Marxist literary
critic Terry Eagleton writes, "Capitalism's reverential hat-tipping to the

arts is obvious hypocrisy, except when it can hang them on its walls as a sound investment" (200). Brushing aside the Straw-man argument that capitalists only care about monetary gain, what Eagleton and his colleagues do not understand (or choose to ignore) is how capitalism, and most especially how the Austrian School, draws a correlation between personal autonomy, artistic ingenuity, and the evaluative act of literary criticism itself. Paul Cantor summarizes the Austrian perspective's interconnection with the arts:

> We argue that this brand of economics, which focuses on the freedom of the individual actor and the subjectivity of values, is more suited to the study of literature and artistic creativity than a materialist, determinist, and collectivist doctrine. The Austrian School is the most humane form of economics we know, and the most philosophically informed—hence we regard it as the most relevant to humanistic studies. (x)

The anti-capitalist approach tends to view economics by way of the producer's authority, whereas the Austrian School views economics through the values of the consumer. To thoroughly examine the intersection of literature and economics, we must "consider capitalism as more complex than the narrow Marxist reduction of capitalism to a system of commodity production" (Berman 185). This is precisely what an Austrian form of capitalist literary criticism can accomplish. Marx himself was amazed at the power of the Industrial Revolution, believing it to represent the machinery of society itself, whereby individuals relinquish their personal autonomy to economic mechanization and are driven to consume because of the impetus of production. (Machinery and production will be addressed in a literary context in chapter 6.) But this analysis lacks understanding of market forces. "Severing the understanding of production from the understanding of consumption is one of the chief defects of Marxist thinking," Cantor writes. "It means that Marxists fail to understand how the market operates as a feedback mechanism, allowing consumers to send signals to producers that guide their business plans" (67–68). In an effort to continually force a collectivist paradigm on the writing, publishing, and reading of literature, anti-capitalists appear to have forgotten that those involved in the literary process are still individuals first and foremost. This leads to incomplete comprehension of not only economics, but of the economics inherent to reading, writing, and to literary criticism itself. Cantor writes, "In contrast to Austrian economists, they have closed their eyes to the individuality of producers and consumers" (70–71).

Marxist critic Raymond Williams writes, "At the very center of Marxism is an extraordinary emphasis on human creativity and self-creation," and such creativity should have "a specific affinity with Marxism" (206). But those with a capitalistic sensibility would argue that it is the market, not Marxism, that promotes and defends individuality and innovation. Stanford scholar Russell Berman, in *Fiction Sets You Free*, examines the connection between a free-market environment and literary creativity, autonomy, and productivity. While everyone is admittedly influenced by their environment on some level, no one is bound to it on some inevitable, pre-determined path, especially those involved in artistic endeavors. The fictional nature of literature, produced by humans' inherent imaginations, allows for creation beyond the political, social, economic, or any other real-world constraints that appear to inhibit us. This separation of literature from a constructed framework reflects the very independence of humanity itself (Berman xi). If one were to posit, as anti-capitalist critics do, that artistic creation is simply the result of capitalistic ideology and reproduction, then one would have to admit that capitalism actually promotes artistic freedom, because any art that contradicts prevailing trends would be impossible without its inherent marketability. Literature and capitalism work together to develop a market for artistic creativity that not only (re)produces autonomy, but also leads to the evolutionary quality of literature that is inextricably bound with democracy (183). Art is dynamic, and challenging, and progressive *because* of capitalism, not in spite of it.

Authors and readers of literature alike also tend to adhere to basic market forces in their respective activities. Authors continually respond to the public and to the works of their contemporaries according to market mechanisms. And this does not lead to "reducing the work to the presumably low level of the public (as an elite criticism would have it)" (Berman 184). Rather, the free market allows for the evolution of taste, thus literary criticism. While economics is usually the study of available options regarding limited resources, literature elicits action by the reader—"the need to choose among the surplus of imaginary possibilities." Through textual analysis, the reader can interpret literature in a number of differing, yet legitimate, ways. Each reader may reach a unique and valid conclusion, choosing whatever elucidation works most coherently for his own enjoyment or understanding. Those available options form the foundation of the development of criticism and taste, and they permit (and encourage) the reader to engage in the exercise of economic choice (187). Berman continues:

> Imaginative literature therefore addresses the reader as an economic actor defined in two complementary ways: as the potentially entrepreneurial visionary who might creatively pursue the realization of the abundance present initially only in the imagination, and as the deliberative and selective consumer, sorting through multiple offerings the help of taste and judgment and therefore potentially prepared for the complexity of market decisions. The economic categories inherent in literature, following from the standing of imagination, are therefore imaginative entrepreneurship (as visionary) and evaluation (as deliber-

ative selection). These are furthermore dimensions of the capitalist economy that the reductionist model of commodity production largely ignores. (187–88)

Capitalistic theory will offer an enlightened perspective of literature. Whereas anti-capitalist criticisms and other similar cultural theories are reductive by nature, often simply providing a grid system that crudely applies to literature, a capitalist criticism is not nearly so deterministic. Operating with other forms of criticism, the reader already knows the answer, as it were: the man is oppressing the woman, the rich is oppressing the poor, the West is oppressing the East, and so on. Applying these inevitable theories gives the reader no legitimate room for discovery. Such predictable forms of criticism simply allow the reader to discover what she already wants to find or be illuminated to what she already believes. Capitalist criticism will serve a higher purpose—to encourage the reader to discover a multitude of interpretations based upon a variety of forms of investigation. The capitalist critic, indeed, may ultimately arrive at the same conclusion as an anti-capitalist or feminist or postcolonial critic, but the option is always available that she may not. Her economic, historical, and logical methodology may lead her elsewhere.

Before exploring where these methods may lead, however, let us return to the philosophical foundation of theory and see how it relates to the economics of capitalism. Theory, in its very nature, is capitalistic. As explained above, it is the formulation of an idea, which is then put into practice, not unlike any tool used by any laborer. The idea is intellectual capital that the theorist may employ according to her needs or goals in an attempt to produce something new, that is, an innovative methodology of reading. Furthermore, the resulting argumentation of the theorist is capitalistic in nature because the theorist must present the theory in the marketplace of ideas. The theorist must defend her position just as any producer must convince her consumers of the acceptability or effectiveness of her particular product in relation to all other products. Certainly, the theorist attempts to profit from this new theory, either in the form of respect from the academy or through monetary gains among the general public. Reputations, and subsequent opportunities for employment, advancement, or payment are founded upon the development of the new product—the theory.

Some will subscribe to the notion that a theorist's grand plan for theorizing, similar to an author's planning of a novel, is rooted in central planning that more closely resembles a socialistic foundation. However, though this is partially accurate, the new theory originates from the individual, must survive in the minds and actions of other individuals, and often is adjusted according to the wants and needs not of the creator, but more importantly of the audience, or receivers of the theory. For example, a theorist who desperately wants to become published or attain tenure will consciously tailor her theory—while still being innovative—according to the ideologies of those she wishes to impress or from whom she wishes to profit. Intellectual capital quickly becomes social capital. This is no different than Steve Jobs having the master plan for the iPad, yet being forced to recognize the potentiality and receptiveness of the market. Jobs had to adjust his designs to fit the desires of those to whom he wanted to sell. Similarly, the theorist undoubtedly aims to present her idea with the predetermination that her notion will be understood, accepted, and adopted. The anti-capitalist theorist, therefore, could be considered a willfully ignorant thinker because she is either unaware of her relation to or deceitfully ideological in her involvement in the very capitalistic process she claims to abhor. A new, capitalistic form of criticism simply aims to bring to light the fundamental nature of theory that has gone ignored for generations—that the development of theory is an intrinsically capitalistic process, and those angered by the capitalistic process are likely to be those most manifestly entrenched in it.

If capitalism is the pursuit of self-interest, resulting in the subsequent benefit for others, then theorizing is perhaps the most capitalistic endeavor imaginable. A theorist will likely investigate something new that fits with her own beliefs or ideology, thus giving her joy. The production of that theory, while still joyful to the theorist, is intended to bring joy to others, particularly when theories of cultural criticism or social justice are proffered. Proclaiming such ideas as themselves inherently progressive, socialistic, or otherwise altruistic is often misleading. As the theorist becomes more successful upon the public accommodation of her theory, everyone else benefits from the increased knowledge and perspective. The pursuit of self-interest with either the hopeful intent or fortunate byproduct of benefiting others is capitalistic, indeed. One could argue that, very much like an entrepreneur, a theorist aims to increase productivity within her specific field, and thus, opportunities for profits (publishing, jobs, promotions, etc.), by altering the division of labor. Inspiring others to accept, expand upon, and succeed from the creation and evolution of, say, feminist theory or post-colonial theory, is a primary effort of the theorist. This is precisely what a business-owner tries to do every day at her factory, bank, retail store, or anywhere else. Because capitalism aims to benefit all, it is very close in purpose to literary theory. If a theorist did not have a goal of helping others to read, think, and write in new and interesting ways for the benefit of not only their own education but for all society, she would never develop the theory.

Creativity, therefore, in both artistic production and in artistic criticism, is entrepreneurial, thus capitalistic. Austrian School economist and entrepreneurship expert Israel Kirzner sees "market capitalism . . . as an ongoing *process of creative discovery*" (ix). An individual as entrepreneur, while attempting to maximize gains through calculations of risk and benefit, ultimately participates in a market economy as a means of exploration of what can potentially be achieved, based on an impetus of creative innovation. The urge to produce creatively precedes the act of production. In other words, for our literary purposes here, a truly entrepreneurial author does not sit at a desk and say to himself, "Time to be creative and write something interesting!" Rather, Kirzner writes, "He has not 'deployed' his hunch for a specific purpose; *rather his hunch has propelled him. . . .* Entrepreneurship is thus not something to be deliberately introduced into a potential production process: it is, instead, something primordial to the very idea of a potential production process awaiting possible implementation" (22). The wonderful result of creativity as capitalism is its ability to spread beyond the initial stage of innovation. When attempting to institute these aims, Kirzner writes, "market participants notice, again, further market possibilities that had hitherto escaped attention. And so on. The process is kept continuously boiling by the incessant injection of unexpected changes and surprises. The process of creative discovery is never completed, nor is it ever arrested" (ix–x). Placing authorship and criticism into a capitalist methodology, in contrast to the vague and reductive social construction notions of anti-capitalist methodologies, provides a deeper understanding of the creative process than is traditionally offered in economic literary readings.

The acts of literary creation and literary criticizing are also undertaken only by individuals, thus leading us to the second fundamental premise of a capitalist economic literary criticism. Ralph Raico, a historian of liberalism, writes that traditional, as well as many current forms of neoclassical, economic methods ignore the complexity of humanity in favor of mathematical models which tend to undermine the "alertness, inventiveness, fallibility, and resourceful creativity of all the participants in the market process" (8–9). Unlike anti-capitalist methods, which place human action as part of a larger collectivist system, Austrians believe in the authority of the individual as acting agent. Austrian economist F. A. Hayek explores this tenet most clearly. He relates that few other terms have been "so abused and misunderstood" as individualism, as it "has been distorted by its opponents into an unrecognizable caricature" (*Individualism* 3). Hayek, and others in the Austrian tradition, place true individualism in the historical tradition of John Locke, David Hume, Edmund Burke, Alexis de Tocqueville, and Lord Acton. This is not to be confused with another form of individualism that developed in French thought from Descartes through Rousseau, which eventually morphed into socialistic and collectivistic ideologies (4). Hayek states that true individualism is simply "a theory of society, an attempt to understand the forces which determine the social life of man." While anti-capitalists tend to view human character as determined by its placement amid social constructs, the individualist methodology argues that "there is no other way toward an understanding of social phenomena but through our understanding of individual actions directed toward other people and guided by their expected behavior" (6).

The individualist perspective often raises two understandable criticisms, which I will address here. First, this position in no way implies that Austrians perceive humans to be isolated from and untouched by the realities of social existence. They simply acknowledge that groups, nations, cultural institutions, and other social entities are still composed of individuals. A group does not have a collective brain with which to make decisions; it has a collection of many brains that individually decide their role of participation in the group. "At the heart of Austrian economics," Cantor writes, "is the idea that human life is filled with social processes, but that these processes still take place among individuals and are rooted in individual preferences and decisions—and hence in human intentionality" (75). Second, individualism does not refer to an all-knowing, rational agent of economic action—a *homo economicus*—that only seeks to maximize self-interest in a mathematical approximation of equilibrium. Austrians acknowledge, and embrace, the complicated and often irrational nature of humanity. It is this complexity of humanity that leads economists from this perspective to disavow large scale prediction and planning. Therefore, the individual must be left to choose for herself, and we as critics or social scientists are left studying those specific implications, subsequent interactions, and larger ramifications. A Marxist philosophy, Mises writes, promotes the opposite approach:

> Marxism asserts that a man's thinking is determined by his class affiliation. Every social class has a logic of its own. The product of thought cannot be anything else than an "ideological disguise" of the selfish class interests of the thinker. It is the task of a "sociology of knowledge" to unmask philosophies and scientific theories and to expose their "ideological" emptiness. Economics is a "bourgeois" makeshift; the economists are "sycophants" of capital. (*Human Action* 5)

From the literary perspective, critic John Carey questions the reductionist labels applied to large groups of people, "variously designated the middle classes or the bourgeoisie," and indicates that such a collectivist methodology is antithetical to the individualist nature of the author or critic:

> What this intellectual effort failed to realize was that the masses do not exist. The mass, that is to say, is a metaphor for the unknowable and the invisible. We cannot see the mass. Crowds can be seen; but the mass is the crowd in its metaphysical aspect—the sum of all possible crowds—and that can take on conceptual form only as a metaphor. The metaphor of the mass serves the purposes of individual self-assertion because it turns other people into a conglomerate. It denies them the individuality which we ascribe to ourselves and to people we know. (*The Intellectuals* 21)

In contrast, it is the emphasis on individuality and its embrace of human complexity that defines this new form of economic literary criticism.

Rather than placing human beings into boxes according to race, gender, class, or some other social construction, and representing them as abstract stand-ins for real, acting people, the Austrian method aims to recognize the complications of life as evidenced through the actions of purposeful individuals. "The emphasis on freedom and individualism in the Austrian School," Cantor writes, "means that when we analyze authors in an economic context, we do not treat them as representatives of a particular ideology, class consciousness, or historical moment. We look at each author as an individual and seek for his or her distinctive ideas" (xvi). Thus, it represents "the very opposite of a deterministic doctrine" (20). One would think such a method, based on freedom, individuality, and creativity, would be "more attractive than the collectivism of Marxism to scholars in the humanities" (19). New York University economist Peter J. Boettke adds, "Individuals and their choice-making activity serve as the beginning of the Austrian analysis not because of a rejection of collective entities, but because it is only by interpreting such social entities as the composite outcome of individual activity that we can come to understand their meaning and significance" (27). The most important idea here is that if literature is intended to reflect a version of reality, then it would behoove us to employ a technique of literary criticism that best understands and explains the messiness of reality. Yes, everyone is influenced by his or her environment, but that influence only goes so far, and real life is governed by real individuals who make very real choices. Even those most physically bound and forcefully constrained, such as those enslaved (as I shall indicate in chapter 2 on Frederick Douglass), still have the power to live as individuals making free choices. Such is the aim of Austrian economics—to seek the power of the individual regardless of the larger social circumstances. Rather than dealing with anti-capitalist notions of vague classes and theoretical (yet unattainable) models of perfection or idealism, Austrians instead focus on individuals and the many complexities that they inhabit. Raico notes, "Individuality bears an intimate, perhaps even logical connection to diversity, and Austrianism, in contrast to neoclassical economics, likewise accentuates the role of diversity in economic life" (11). Thus, tackling literature in light of all of the difficulties of real life would potentially and logically produce a more appropriate and effective criticism.

Following the inherent capitalistic nature of both theory and creativity, as well as privileging the fundamental role of the individual as both a creative and economic agent, the third quality we must acknowledge in a capitalist literary criticism concerns the concept of subjective value. It is one of the primary tenets of Austrian economics, and it is a principal argument against the traditional belief in the labor theory of value, as introduced by classical economists like Adam Smith and David Ricardo and subsequently embraced by Marx. The dispute between the objective and the subjective is a long-standing one and demonstrates the illogical nature of most anti-capitalist literary criticism. Cantor writes that

> It is one of the many ironies of literary criticism today that postmodernists, who deny all objectivity, have linked up with Marxism, a form of economics rooted in the labor theory of value, which seeks to determine value on the basis of an objective factor. The fact that Austrian economics clearly acknowledges that all economic value is purely subjective is one reason why it should be more attractive to literary critics than Marxism as an economic theory. (9)

A literary criticism rooted in Austrian capitalism is a much more consistently coherent form of economic analysis of literature, because literature, even more than many realms of life, is an activity and object filled with the judgments of subjective value.

The economics of this connection to literature is thoroughly described by Mises and other Austrians in their definitions of valuation. They describe how products can only be arranged according to preference—an inherent "quantity or magnitude of value" does not exist. Thus, a sum of values (as indicated in the labor theory) is absurd. Mises writes, "It would be nonsensical to assert that the value attached to a product is equal to the 'sum' of the values attached to the various complementary factors of production. One cannot add up values or valuations" (*Human Action* 332). Goods have value simply because individuals have chosen to deem them valuable based on preferences over time. Such is the case with literature and other art. The entire movement away from formalistic literary criticism is predicated upon a subjective theory of value. No longer do critics seek an inherently valuable aspect of text; no longer is there a "correct" method for crafting literature. A capitalist form of criticism makes sense because value in literature is determined just as all other products are valued: subjectively. Capitalist literary criticism allows the critic to determine for herself, using her own free will, educated analysis, and artistic spirit the value of a piece of literature. Anti-capitalism criticism, once again, simply applies a formula, rather than looking at true, economically subjective forces.

Subjective value also provides flexibility within the heated debates about the canon and canon formation. As one of the more controversial and purposeful goals of literary critics of all stripes is to expand the literary canon to include works by marginalized authors who work in marginalized forms, we should note that a capitalistic perspective is equally conducive to this expansion based on the premise of subjective value. A capitalist form of criticism is most certainly not based upon a "conservative" mentality whereby only Greek classics and Shakespearean Renaissance pieces and other traditional works of the Western canon, developed and reified predominantly by white males, are the only works of value. This theory could not be further from that position: this perspective is not one in which classical ideals are upheld as representing only forms of "good" literature, and does not believe that we must regurgitate such works in order to perpetuate literature and its traditions. Capitalist criticism simply does not care which works are examined, and it has no preference for which works eventually become canonized. Where a text resides within the tradition of literature and its accompanying criticism is of very little concern. As this criticism resides on the very foundation of cultural *evolution*, it cannot support such a traditionalist methodology. While this dispassionate approach may bring curiosity as to why a capitalist critic would bother examining canonization at all, we must remember that the very act of choosing, labeling, classifying, and sharing is itself economic. The dissemination of information regarding preference or importance is the foundation of the free market. Whether such information regarding texts is then proliferated and accepted is to be determined, but the very process reaffirms that an act like canonizing is imbedded within cultural evolution, according to an Austrian methodology.

Each of these fundamental facets of Austrian economics—entrepreneurism, individualism, and subjectivism—will appear in each of the following chapters either by way of the voice and perspective of the author or through the respective characters they create. The literary works selected for study here offer wonderful examples of the complexity of the nature of individuals and the diverse, and often difficult, interactions that result from their human fallibility. Theory is not an abstract, existing separate from reality. It is based on humanity and the phenomenon of existence and how the two relate to one another. The resulting action is intentional and directional, undertaken by humans making value judgments toward specific conclusions. Theory requires an observation of the essences of humanity and reality in order for humans to choose how to function in reality. Therefore, theory is never isolated from the humanity it describes; and if it is legitimate, it is inherently applicable. If a theory cannot effectively be used pragmatically, then there is no purpose for the theory and no way to measure its quality as a theory. Therefore, we only develop what we believe to be practical. And capitalism is the very essence of what it means to function practically in the real world and marketplace.

Theory must acknowledge that it is always missing various (and often large) portions of information in its analysis of and application to literature. Capitalist criticism, by its introduction or existence, does not seek to refute this premise; thus, if it did, it would be as guilty as all other forms of theory. On the contrary, this form of criticism readily admits that it, too, is not an all-knowing authority on literary analysis. Rather, it simply seeks to provide more information about and better analysis of existing sources. It is just offering the capitalist an economically theoretical story of the text. As Cantor explains, "The Austrian School respects the heterogeneity of phenomena and hence of a variety of methods of studying them. The Austrians do not accept the idea of a master science, one method of knowing that provides the key to understanding all phenomena" (19). In contrast to anti-capitalist criticisms, the aim of the economics of this theory is not to explain "why" economic actions occur and thus plan for the future accordingly; rather the capitalist economic perspective simply explains that certain economic actions in fact do occur, and that they are largely based upon the deficiencies of individuals and human nature itself instead of large and vague notions of systems, structures, and classes. Therefore, it is not directing anyone toward future behavior; it is simply analyzing previous economic behavior for what it is.

One need not be an expert in literary jargon to explore this form of criticism, because it is not based upon an elite class of individuals determining who their authorities are and who can speak for such a perspective. In capitalist criticism, since it is open to the free market and to each individual's personal expertise, anyone should be able to understand and contribute to its analysis of literature and its advancement in cultural discourse. In that manner, capitalist criticism is much more egalitarian than traditional anti-capitalist theories. We emphasize competing theories, a variety of historically verified facts, and diverse interpretations. Capitalist criticism decentralizes theory and deregulates its participants' methods. Therefore, in this form, one will see a wide variety of sources used in citation, as analysis is drawn from the expertise of many individuals (with real world experience) rather than solely from the theoretical knowledge (no matter how advanced or respected) of a few academics. My method will be to proceed by drawing analysis from actual economists and historians, not those pretending to such knowledge based on their vague notions of what affects economics or history.

Though I personally take a keen interest in American literature, and focus on it exclusively in this book, this is certainly not to say that a capitalist literary criticism must only pertain to American literature or to a specific genre or form. Capitalist themes can clearly be found throughout world literature as well, in the Russian works of Aleksandr Solzhenitsyn, or in the works of renowned Peruvian Mario Vargas Llosa. Paul Cantor has also written extensively on German author Thomas Mann. Because capitalism involves individual economic actions, an author or text need not reside in traditionally capitalistic societies to receive an Austrian economic literary treatment.

British literature is also a fertile area for capitalist economic analysis. Daniel Defoe's *Robinson Crusoe*, the 1719 British novel that was perhaps the world's first bestseller, has as its namesake a vital element to the study of economics in classical, neoclassical, and Austrian traditions. "Robinson Crusoe economics" was first identified by Karl Marx, as he briefly used the novel to explain his belief in the intrinsic value of labor over capital. That notion was later challenged by capitalists such as Austrian economists who instead presented the novel alongside discussions of such technical concepts as the regression theorem, Pareto efficiency, and comparative advantage.

Another canonical British author, Charles Dickens, has begun to receive capitalist consideration. Studies of Dickens have started to evolve from the standard belief that the prominent British author was an unwavering advocate for the poor and critic of industrial capitalism in Victorian England. In addition to the varied interpretation of *A Christmas Carol* that I posited above, which is supported by NYU professor Bruce Bueno de Mesquita in his clever book, *The Trial of Ebenezer Scrooge*, other Dickens works are receiving second looks from an economic perspective. Author Sarah Skwire has recently begun to promote a capitalist interpretation of Dickens based on the capitalist protagonists and prominence of business compared to the harsh depictions of government institutions and criminal enterprises of many of his works, such as *Oliver Twist, Bleak House, Great Expectations, Little Dorrit, David Copperfield*, and others. Cantor, in *Literature and the Economics of Liberty*, has extensively examined Dickens's publishing process from a free-market economic perspective, demonstrating that not only can a text explore capitalistic themes, but the very process of creating that text can be analyzed through a capitalist lens, as well.

Even Shakespeare can receive the capitalist treatment. Shakespeare often employed economic terminology for the effect of multiple meanings, as indicated in Frederick Turner's *Shakespeare's Twenty-First Century Economics*, but we also see the author's placement of characters and narrative amid very real economic conditions. Though "capitalism" had not yet been clearly defined, capitalist economic trends can be found in many of the Bard's works. In one extended example, let us briefly look at a capitalist re-reading of *The Merchant of Venice*. There are, of course, myriad economic representations in this play (from the legal framework of the time and Venetian commerce, to the economics of religion, marriage, and more), so I shall only highlight one here. Examining the role of Shylock as usurer and how his contract with Antonio is crafted allows, in a free-market economic criticism, a much different interpretation from the traditional anti-capitalist view. An anti-capitalist economic criticism relies upon an upper or middle class making money (or in this case, extracting flesh) on the labors of those without access to capital, thereby profiting without laboring. The ability for money to create money is an exploitative practice only available to those in power or seeking it, who continue to perpetuate the capitalist economic system for their own increased wealth. Consequently, the debtor, through not only borrowing but through interest, is enslaved to the creditor and will remain in a subservient class. On the other hand, an anti-capitalist reading might also point out that Antonio is not of a lower class, but rather of the wealthy merchant class. Shylock, thus, stands for the rising bourgeoisie, seeking to displace the quasi-aristocratic landowners and commercialists. In either case, class is a vital component for an anti-capitalist analysis of this play and for providing harsh judgment of Shylock.

Alternatively, a free-market economic criticism offers a possible redemption for Shylock. The basic principles of a true, free-market exchange are very simple: one is not allowed to defraud, coerce or threaten, steal from, or inflict harm upon an unwilling other; and the transaction shall be considered beneficial to each party involved. Shylock and Antonio, of their own free will, design and agree upon a clearly stated contract in which both men know the consequences for default. This financial transaction is not about "values" or "morals"; true freedom of commerce is always based upon subjective value. We may find the deal that has been made repugnant, but no economic principles have been broken. No one has forced Antonio into his dangerous bargain. Further, they both see the exchange as beneficial—Antonio obtains an opportunity to help his friend, and Shylock is given the chance to exact a form of punishment for being continuously abused by Antonio and his ilk. Shylock is the one taking the risk as the lender; therefore, the penalty he requires is based on two factors regarding the potential for moral hazard on the part of current and future debtors. Mises explains:

> The lender is always faced with the possibility that he may lose a part or the whole of the principal lent. His appraisal of this danger determines his conduct in bargaining with the prospective debtor about the terms of the contract. . . . He can be affected by changes in the market data concerning them. He has linked his fate with that of the debtor or with the changes occurring in the price of the collateral. (*Human Action* 536)

First, since Shylock is the one taking the financial risk (after all, if a borrower defaults, it is not the borrower's livelihood in jeopardy—it is the creditor's), he must make the interest valuable enough that it is worth his loaning out the principal in the short term and ensuring that future borrowers will not take advantage of him in the long term. Second, due to the abhorrent behavior inflicted upon Jews in the play, including Antonio's own vile and unrepentant actions toward Shylock, Shylock must propose a penalty in which Antonio will "feel" the consequences of breaking the contract. Since Antonio is already wealthy, a higher interest rate is likely not enough compulsion. Shylock chooses physical punishment in order to force Antonio to consider carefully the gravity of not only borrowing a large sum of money, but also of pleading for assistance from a man he only recently spat upon. Shylock is insuring his investment as a lender, but also, as a Jew, seeking human dignity and respect.

The fact that Antonio is not a member of the underclass, but rather has vast investments, actually situates him as representative of the majority of debtors throughout history. What many forget is that free-market capitalism actually altered the constituency of those who comprise the roles of creditors and debtors: "The masses of people with more moderate income are rather themselves creditors. On the other hand, the rich . . . are more often debtors than creditors. In asking for the expropriation of creditors, the masses are unwittingly attacking their own particular interests" (Mises, *Human Action* 537–38). Though stigmatized, usury plays the beneficial role of putting capital into the hands of those who need it in the short term and who would otherwise not be able to engage in economic action. The fact that someone makes money through interest on the back end is excellent for an economy because such an incentive moves capital from those who do not immediately need it for investment or expenditures to those who do. Therefore, capitalism has the capability of inverting class distinctions, providing improved economic opportunities and circumstances for all levels of wealth.

Literary critics and anti-capitalist economists have historically shaped the argument regarding the topic of debt. Mises explains, "Public opinion has always been biased against creditors. It identifies creditors with the idle rich and debtors with the industrious poor. It abhors the former as ruthless exploiters and pities the latter as innocent victims of oppression (*Human Action* 537). And art aids in shaping that public opinion better than nearly every other cultural institution. To this day, Shylock (and other businessmen of literature) still embodies the link between usury and evil, despite the fact that such an economic perspective has long since expired. However, a more thorough examination of the realities of economics allows the opportunity for an entirely different literary critique. The Shylock of anti-capitalism is a man shaped by greed and maliciousness and revenge. In a new form of economic criticism, Shylock is regarded as an honest investor who, while simply seeking payment on a fully-consented contract in order to protect his livelihood, is victimized by a legal loophole (which is argued under deceitful conditions) that contradicts the agreed-upon intent and understanding of the contract between two responsible adults. Thus, if we only view Shylock or the concepts of debt, contract agreement, or default within the boundaries of Shakespeare's play, rather than in relation to economic life and philosophy in general, we are neglecting important elements and potential insights in literary analysis.

University of California Berkeley scholar Frederick Crews writes, "I value singular departures from established belief and practice, even when those efforts produce clouded results. The best American novelists have themselves been liberal in this sense, courting isolation and incoherence in the hope of making something new" (xxi). My push for a capitalist economic criticism and reexamination of American literature reflects Crews's values. Crews himself was a contrarian in the field of psychoanalytic criticism. Anytime something new is proposed, the conclusions drawn may appear to reside on shaky ground, but it is the attempt at innovation that signifies progress. Very aware of his own contrarian place in literary criticism, Cantor understands the hesitancy to adapt to a new form of literary criticism, and places the culpability on the hegemonic practices of entrenched anti-capitalist critics and professors. "Much that we argue may initially sound strange," he writes, "but that is just one more sign of how dominant the Marxist paradigm has become in the humanities in recent decades and how it has limited the horizons of what passes for legitimate scholarly discourse on literature and economics" (xviii). While enlightening the reader regarding economic concepts, this capitalist form of economic literary criticism allows the opportunity for not only individual works to be interpreted, but for bringing the very concept of literature under scrutiny.

Economics may also help us to understand more clearly particular forms of literature. Genres and styles evolve, reacting to and improving upon one another, according to capitalistic processes whereby authors are encouraged to either produce texts according to public demand, or break from social norms like an adventurous entrepreneur in order to craft new and imaginative art that takes public opinion in a different direction. Economics may also help us to understand more clearly particular forms of literature, such as the novel. The free-market economy based on competition (and specifically the spontaneous order theory in capitalism) can illuminate the evolution of the novel as a burgeoning literary form in the nineteenth century, in which "popular" fiction excelled, just as did those works which we now call "classics," such as those of Charles Dickens. The marketplace provided not only fun and frivolous literature, but also great works that are still considered high standards of artistic invention. Free individuals and entrepreneurs can be intimately involved with the production of not only public pleasure, but valuable art. Within those texts, characters are allowed to change, depending on the economics applied. A villain in an anti-capitalist interpretation can be transformed into a hero through a capitalist analysis, and vice versa. Even literary value and the concept of criticism itself are assisted through economic understandings of subjective value or marginal utility. The fundamental characteristics of literature are thus allowed to become more fluid and engaging, rather than prescribed and stagnant. The interplay between literature and economics, I believe, offers the ultimate experience in intellectual pleasure: the opportunity for constant surprise.

Ultimately, once the deceptive visions of capitalism that have been propagated by anti-capitalist literary critics have been properly challenged and refuted, the Austrian School corresponds to literary creation in a rather obvious fashion. The importance of freedom and individualism are as vital to the artistic process as they are to the democratic process and to human action in total. Connecting our liberty with our literature is what a capitalist literary criticism can provide that various forms of anti-

sciousness " (McLellan 425). Ultimately, Marx writes, "Production by isolated individuals outside society . . . is as great an absurdity as the idea of the development of language without individuals living together and talking to one another" (*Grundrisse* 17–18). In keeping with this comparison, however, language must still be spoken by a "first person" — someone, an individual, still had to choose to make the first meaningful sound. Everything, even something as social as language, begins with an individual.

Austrian economist Ludwig von Mises responds to Marx's critique of individualism by first acknowledging that, of course, humans are always connected to the rest of humanity and exist as a member of a societal framework: "It is uncontested that in the sphere of human action social entities have real existence. Nobody ventures to deny that nations, states, municipalities, parties, religious communities, are real factors determining the course of human events" (*Human Action* 42). Therefore, we must more clearly understand the aims of analyzing economic action from an individualist perspective. "Methodological individualism," he writes, "far from contesting the significance of such collective wholes, considers it as one of its main tasks to describe and to analyze their becoming and disappearing, their changing structures, and their operation" (42). Mises explains that, while social entities certainly affect our lives, those social entities are made up of individuals, and no social group can exist apart from the individual actions of its constituents (42). Once we are able to identify the starting point of all economic action as emanating from the individual, we are then able to analyze that individual's specific actions.

The actions of all individuals always signify the pursuit of some purposeful end.

Referencing the philosophy of John Locke, Mises writes,

> Acting man is eager to substitute a more satisfactory state of affairs for a less satisfactory. His mind imagines conditions which suit him better, and his action aims at bringing about this desired state. The incentive that impels a man to act is always some uneasiness. A man perfectly content with the state of affairs would have no incentive to change things. . . . But to make a man act, uneasiness and the image of a more satisfactory state alone are not sufficient. A third condition is required: the expectation that purposeful behavior has the power to remove or at least to alleviate the felt uneasiness. In the absence of this condition no action is feasible. (13–14)

From this philosophical perspective, we can begin to see how Frederick Douglass fits within the terminology of economic action, as indicated by the Austrian School's understanding of capitalism.

Douglass, though enduring a horrific existence of enslavement, remains an acting individual whose life choices, though severely limited due to his abhorrent circumstances, are still varied and available. As difficult as it may seem to an outsider considering his personal story and the historical realities of slavery, Douglass (and all other humans) constantly maintains the power to choose among various options. And the economic agent will always choose methods of improving one's existence as one sees fit and accessible. These methods often become known by observing the surrounding world, as we will soon see Douglass do throughout his text. A human often "chooses to adopt traditional patterns or patterns adopted by other people because he is convinced that this procedure is best fitted to achieve his own welfare" Mises writes. "And he is ready to change his ideology and consequently his mode of action whenever he becomes convinced that this would better serve his own interests" (46). Contrary to Marx's determinist views of social action, whenever an individual "discovers that the pursuit of the habitual way may hinder the attainment of ends considered as more desirable, he changes his attitude" (47). It is the constant adjustment to surrounding models of action that defines an individual's pursuit of particular ends. And it is through changing one's own personal qualities—and thus, economic opportunities—that human capital is acquired and employed.

As we are discussing the institution of slavery in this chapter, we must distinguish between human capital as a result of the productivity of enslaved persons and human capital as the individual, self-willed result of rational improvement toward one's own ends. The former reflects a capital good, like machinery, which is simply a tool for increasing the profits of the owner of that capital good. This is completely unacceptable in Austrian capitalism, as the owner of the labor, the slave, is not allowed to prosper through free trade of service or production; thus, along with the use of force implicit in slavery, among many other dehumanizing abuses, this definition of human capital is not what signifies true, free-market capitalism. On the other hand, the latter definition of human capital, which will be employed here, whereby any individual has the power to improve oneself according to one's own goals and desires, is entirely representative of Douglass's pursuit of an improved life.

Douglass himself was an occasional critic of capitalism not only for its connection to slavery, but also for its influence on the wages of free workers. Douglass was very concerned about laborers receiving low wages and the resulting class divides, and attributed this to the perceived conflict between capital and labor. He once stated, "Experience demonstrates that there may be a slavery of wages only a little less galling and crushing in its effects than chattel slavery" (qtd. in Martin 128). However, this is not a damning indictment of capitalism, as all workers want to be paid more; such a complaint is practically axiomatic from a laborer's perspective. And the Austrian theory of capitalism has no problem with workers independently organizing and negotiating for higher wages, or simply moving on to look for more advantageous employment. While concerned about workers, Douglass actually "criticized trade unions for

pathway became much more smooth than before; my condition was now much more comfortable." But being a respected laborer and earning a living made him crave freedom even more strongly: "I have observed this in my condition of slavery—that whenever my condition was improved, instead of its increasing my contentment, it only increased my desire to be free, and set me to thinking of plans to gain my freedom" (64).

When Douglass had to give up nearly all of his earnings to his master, his urge for independence increased further. He knew the profit he earned was rightfully his, as he had contracted for it and labored honestly for it. But he had to deliver that money to a master that, as he describes, had no right to it, "solely because he had the power to compel" Douglass to relinquish it (65). By 1838, giving up his hard-earned wages had brought him to a tipping point. And when his master would give him a few cents in commission as a reward, Douglass was just further angered: "It had the opposite effect. I regarded it as a sort of admission of my right to the whole" (66). He determined to hire himself out to earn enough money to make his escape. He was able to make a financial arrangement, but he knew the work would be painfully difficult, both physically and mentally: "It was a step towards freedom to be allowed to bear the responsibilities of a freeman, and I was determined to hold on upon it. . . . I was ready to work at night as well as day, and by the most untiring perseverance and industry, I made enough to meet my expenses, and lay up a little money every week" (67). Douglass soon learned his master's ability to make money was through Douglass's efforts. Therefore, when his master enforced restrictions, he would go on a personal strike: "I spent the whole week without the performance of a single stroke of work. I did this in retaliation" (68). His master soon got more work for him, and eventually rewarded him more handsomely at the end of the week. But all the while, even more than money, Douglass was thinking of freedom. By September 1838, Douglass fled to New York.

A person willing or able to recognize the correlation among work, incentive, and risk is a person knowledgeable about his or her own human capital. As Douglass later wrote, "We succeed, not alone by the laborious exertions of our faculties, be they small or great, but by the regular, thoughtful and systematic exercise of them" ("Self-Made Men"). Elizabeth Hoyt explains, in a chapter of her book titled "The Nature of Wants," the ability to weigh what an individual wants takes a significant degree of intellectualism, and this perceptiveness is clearly displayed in Douglass. To address a problem, see potential, and then reason through economic decisions, as Douglass did in choosing his escape, requires innate human capital, just as an investor must determine the risks and rewards of a stock purchase. F. A. Hayek writes, "practically every individual has some advantage over all others because he possesses unique information of which beneficial use might be made, but of which use can be made only if the decisions depending on it are left to him or are made with his active co-operation" (521–22). Douglass decided through careful consideration to invest in himself, and his freedom was the ultimate profit. And achieving freedom is yet another addition in Douglass's stockpile of capital because freedom offers increased access and opportunity, like any other acquired skill or quality.

Upon his arrival in the North, though he had previously labored for the sole purpose of earning money for his flight, Douglass learned that working for paltry income or even none at all can also be a way of attaining human capital. A brief anecdote illustrates this point. Shortly after Douglass made his great escape, a poverty-stricken and inept young man named Frank Winfield Woolworth took a job as a sales clerk, working fourteen-hour days for no pay for the first three months. While we may look at this as exploitative, he eventually proved worthy of a salary, which he put toward starting his own store, which eventually would become the famous Woolworth's retail chain. Years later, he even ended up being the boss of his former employer, and became one of the richest men in nineteenth-century America (Sowell, *Applied Economics* 24–25). Though it is often thought of as a progressive social measure, imposing minimum wages on businesses usually deters them from hiring those most in need of developing human capital, the marginalized. Furthermore, "Those who disdain low-paying jobs as 'menial' or who refuse to accept 'chump change' for entry-level work are usually not thinking beyond stage one" (26). Douglass's willingness to take any job available, regardless of the filth or the lack of pay, helped him acquire capital in himself that led to more appealing and prosperous endeavors.

Douglass relates two instances of this in his *Narrative*. The first occurs while he is still a slave down on the wharf in Baltimore, where he voluntarily offered his assistance to two Irish workers. They learned Douglass was a slave and sympathized with him, encouraging him to escape to the North. His voluntary labor not only formed brief acquaintances, but further inspired him to escape. The second case was as a free man in New Bedford. By his third day there, Douglass describes, he had found work "stowing a sloop with a load of oil. It was new, dirty, and hard work for me; but I went at it with a glad heart and a willing hand." And he was able to become proud of himself, perhaps for the first time: "I was now my own master. . . . It was the first work, the reward of which was to be entirely of my own. . . . I worked that day with a pleasure I had never before experienced. I was at work for myself and my newly-married wife." Not even discrimination could stand in his way when he struggled to find employment as a calker: "[I] prepared myself to do any kind of work I could get to do. . . . There was no work too hard—none too dirty. I was ready to saw wood, shovel coal, carry the hod, sweep the chimney, or roll oil casks—all of which I did for three years in New Bedford, before I became known to the anti-slavery world" (74). This ethic was a consistent theme for Douglass, as he describes in "Self-Made Men": "We may explain success mainly by one word and that word is work, work, work, work. . . . Everyone may avail himself of this marvelous power, if he will."

Douglass noticed that in the North nearly everyone did work this way, and everyone reaped the benefits, even fellow blacks. He describes, "Every man appeared to understand his work, and went at it with a sober, yet cheerful earnestness, which betokened the deep interest which he felt in what he was doing, as well as a sense of his own dignity as a man" (72). One of his black friends, Mr. Johnson, "lived in a neater house; dined at a better table; took, paid for, and read, more newspapers; better understood the moral, religious, and political character of the nation, than nine tenths of the slaveholders in Talbot County, Maryland." But Mr. Johnson attained this way of life through employing his personal human capital: "Mr. Johnson was a working man. His hands were hardened by toil, and not his alone, but those also of Mrs. Johnson" (73). Douglass's own fiancée was a free woman who performed domestic jobs, and they were quickly married, as a partnership with a spouse can be a vital supplement to one's human capital. Douglass's hard work allowed him the money to buy and read the abolitionist publication, "The Liberator." This reading expanded his human capital even more, and reified his ideas about the "principles, measures and spirit of the anti-slavery reform" (74). And he took up the fight, becoming the influential public intellectual we remember today.

Douglass's later career as an outspoken abolitionist aligns precisely with the economic principles of reproducing human capital defined by Sowell:

> Economically, the question is how best to make the existing human capital more widely available, so that the less fortunate have more opportunity to achieve higher levels of productivity and consequently higher income. . . . Maximum utilization and dissemination of existing human capital is achieved by incentives that reward those who have it. . . . This induces existing possessors of human capital to use it more extensively for the rewards and—more important in the long run—encourages others to acquire more human capital in order to reap similar rewards. (*The Economics* 249)

Theodore Schultz states that human capital may be measured in "the relation between the returns from additional quality and the cost of acquiring it." He adds, "The value of additional human capital depends on the additional well-being that human beings derive from it" (12). There is no doubt that Douglass's well-being was much improved after his choice to escape. Douglass's improved life in the North, obtained through his own brave efforts, was an incomparable reward for his previously dreadful existence in slavery. This reward was what he believed all men, regardless of color, should have the opportunity to pursue through freedom. And as an author, speaker, and abolitionist, Douglass was unyielding in his mission. He had achieved the pinnacle of human capital through the exertion of highly individualized effort.

Marx's perspective on human capital could not be more different. In the 1867 Preface to *Das Kapital*, Marx writes, "Individuals are dealt with only in so far as they are the personifications of economic categories, embodiments of particular class relations and class interests. My standpoint, from which the evolution of the economic formation of society is viewed as a process of natural history, can less than any other make the individual responsible for relations whose creature he socially remains, however much he may subjectively raise himself above them" (McLellan 454). But Douglass's "deep belief in laissez-faire liberalism" suggests a framework by which anyone, at least those who choose to embrace it, can achieve the dream of self-realization and economic success (qtd. in Martin 256). Douglass claims that those who choose to create value within themselves

> are the men who owe little or nothing to birth, relationship, friendly surroundings; to wealth inherited or to early approved means of education; who are what they are, without the aid of any of the favoring conditions by which other men usually rise in the world and achieve great results. In fact they are the men who are not brought up but who are obliged to come up, not only without the voluntary assistance or friendly cooperation of society, but often in open and derisive defiance of all the efforts of society and the tendency of circumstances to repress, retard, and keep them down. ("Self-Made Men")

Douglass's *Narrative* clearly stands in opposition to Marx's naturalistic beliefs and provides great insight not only into the larger economic conditions of slavery in the nineteenth century, but also for the individualistic economic causes and effects that still exist today. However, the text also accomplishes another important feat. Frederick Douglass's *Narrative* exposes the difficulty in condemning individualism and capitalism, while simultaneously holding high regard for Douglass. As he has shown, even the evils of slavery do not guarantee a life of oppression. The common notion that not everyone can pull themselves up by the bootstraps is countered by the achievements of Douglass's life journey. To press this prevailing metaphor a bit further, not only did Douglass not have straps or even boots; he did not even possess legs. His circumstances were so dire that the very idea of his triumph would border on the absurd if it were not so powerfully true. Douglass's endurance and passion led to investment in his own human capital that took him places where freedom endured, opportunity shone, and success blossomed. His diligent acquisition of human capital, under the worst conditions, eventually landed him remarkable personal power, a power that helped to free millions from bondage. His will to take control of his own life led to the development of human capital for others. Examining human capital through the individualism-inspired methodology of the Austrian School of economic literary criticism allows us to draw text away from the theoretical and towards the practical, and from this critical perspective, Douglass's *Narrative* should be an inspiration to those both with boots and without.

THREE

Gatsby, Daisy, and the Austrian Business Cycle

While F. Scott Fitzgerald was publishing his 1925 masterwork, *The Great Gatsby*, in the middle of an unprecedented boom of prosperity, two men were predicting the economy's inevitable collapse. Austrians Ludwig von Mises and Friedrich Hayek were two of the only economists in the world to foresee the approaching failure of the United States market in 1929 and the ensuing Great Depression of the 1930s. Despite the accuracy of their prediction, their models were subsequently abandoned in favor of the new Keynesian economic theories of the 1930s, and the immense government expansion that they required, realized in the form of New Deal legislation. The Austrian business cycle theory that was so accurate only a few years before was lost to the winds of increasingly popular interventionist economic policy. It took until the twenty-first century, when the recent market tumult reared its head in 2008, that the predictive accuracy of the Austrian theory was once again proven. The theory's foundational premise delineates between individual economic action and outside factors that skew market behavior; such outside factors cause misperceptions in efficacy of and misappropriation in investments. But skewed economic actions are not relegated to financial systems. In this chapter, I will demonstrate that economic conditions provide incentives for action and that misleading information causes misplaced values in all aspects of life—even in the fictional world. In Fitzgerald's novel, we see false market signals that cause characters to pursue foolishly the poor choices that can be accounted for by the Austrian business cycle theory. The interactions between Jay Gatsby and Daisy Buchanan, and specifically his pursuit of her affection, are reflective of a business investment or another economic transaction. The evolution of their relationship, from optimistic highs to depressive lows, from booms to busts, can be compared to the business cycle illustrated by the Austrian School.

But before tackling this broader economic explication, let us briefly review Fitzgerald's text according to more traditional economic readings. *The Great Gatsby* has been analyzed from an economic perspective myriad times. However, the vast majority of such criticisms tend toward anti-capitalist or other cultural studies interpretations in which themes of wealth disparity, class distinctions (like the *nouveau riche*), and other social ills are identified. Ross Posnock offers an intriguing analysis of Fitzgerald's anti-capitalist implications by comparing *The Great Gatsby* to Marx's "Money" essay in his *Economic and Philosophic Manuscripts*; Marx's examination of commodity fetishism in the first volume of *Das Kapital*; and Georg Lukács' re-envisioning of Marx in his famous *History and Class Consciousness*. Posnock contends that in making these textual associations, we may more clearly understand Fitzgerald's own "essentially Marxian" economic perspective and his critical attitude toward capitalist culture (201). Alienation and reification, Posnock writes, define the complications of the flawed realities that Gatsby has constructed for himself and that Nick has constructed for the reader, while blurring the lines between humans and objects, as desires become central to such constructions.

Roger Lewis sees Gatsby's love for Daisy as "formulated in monetary terms," in that "its expression is distinctively that of postwar America, of a society that consumes" (46). He writes that Gatsby's love for Daisy and love of money are so inextricably linked that their relationship cannot exist in a world without money, as Daisy's allure becomes connected to a wealth only Gatsby himself can define and understand. Because Gatsby lives out his love for Daisy based on the past, it is not tainted by their presently complicated economic, social, and moral circumstances: "It exists in the world of money and corruption but is not of it" (48). In contrast to Tom, who does not love Daisy for monetary reasons, Gatsby always sees her in the light of his humble beginnings and continuously equates the attainment of her love with the simultaneous attainment of her status. Gatsby uses his new money purposely to win Daisy, the human manifestation of a dream that Tom or anyone else from old money could never fully comprehend (Lewis 50–51).

In "Possessions in *The Great Gatsby*," Scott Donaldson writes how from jewelry to cars, clothing to dogs, countless items are purchased and possessed, and how each item displays a signification of the character who owns or uses it. Furthermore, not only are objects purchased freely, but so are people's affection and social status. Donaldson describes the famous work of Thorstein Veblen, *The Theory of the Leisure Class*, and its relationship to the presentation of Gatsby and his environment, specifically through terminology like "pecuniary emulation," "conspicuous leisure," and "conspicuous consumption." These ideas of Veblen imply the outward display of wealth not for any productive value, but simply for the sake of display, thereby leading others to engage in similar behaviors of wealth exhibition, specifically by those of lesser means, in an attempt to appear as wealthy as upper classes. Gatsby's lack of inherited wealth, along with his opulent lifestyle, fit Veblen's descriptions accordingly (202–3).

There is certainly merit in these critiques, and I am not necessarily disputing the effectiveness of an anti-capitalist reading. However, there are other elements in this novel that are worth investigating when viewed from an Austrian economic perspective, one in which free-market capitalism is more thoroughly examined, rather than being used as a convenient and misunderstood prop for social condemnation. In this chapter, several principles of Austrian economic philosophy will provide insight into a more diverse and illuminating reading of the novel. To continue with the theme of the previous chapter, we will start by analyzing Gatsby as the embodiment of self-made success, a culmination of human capital that has lifted him from anonymous poverty to greatness.

Overcoming an obscure past with little opportunity for growth, Gatsby undergoes a transformation that symbolizes the foundation of capitalistic economic activity: humans making conscious choices toward improved circumstances. Gatsby did not inherit money from his family, and his life was not defined by lucky breaks. Rather, he remembered what it was like to be broke and unknown, and by force of will, he taught himself to be successful. By changing his name from James Gatz and perpetuating his Oxford-educated persona, he forged a new identity for himself. By keeping a disciplined schedule of athletic exercise, financial prudence, and academic studying, he improved his skills, intelligence, and appearance. By maintaining hygiene, abandoning tobacco, respecting elders, and making efforts to "practice elocution, poise and how to attain it," Gatsby invested in his own likeability and capacity to form social relationships (173). Nick even notices this about Gatsby earlier in the novel: "he had probably discovered that people liked him when he smiled" (100). Adapting to one's surroundings and presenting one's self accordingly mirrors Douglass's method for social climbing discussed in the previous chapter. This individualistic struggle is not only representative of the economic agent, but the American citizen, pursuing a dream that would be unattainable elsewhere in the world. While a reader may not respect the superficial man he has become or the ostentatious environment he inhabits, one must acknowledge Gatsby's path to self-improvement and the tremendous personal initiative and effort undertaken to achieve it. And though the sources of his financial capital remain suspect, his human capital has increased exponentially.

Gatsby also adheres to another key component of the Austrian School of capitalism, the pursuit of subjective value. While anti-capitalists (like esteemed critic Fredric Jameson in *Postmodernism, or, the Cultural Logic of*

Late Capitalism, and others) have a problem with assigning value to intangible or knowledge-based entities (and even signifying value of manufactured, physical entities, for that matter), the Austrian School of economics does not. Lukács states that "Commodity fetishism is a specific problem of our age, the age of modern capitalism," and it is "the central, structural problem of capitalist society of all aspects" (84–85). Though it may appear callous, capitalism simply says, "So what?" to the commodification of social structures and the fetishism of "stuff." The reason is that all things have a subjective value, even non-physical products, and no amount of moral resentment will change this. The reader may object to this behavior according to some religious or other belief system, but in order to remain economically consistent, the reader should not care that Gatsby is trying to buy Daisy's love or prestige in the community.

Those critics that disagree with the commoditization of life must examine the role of subjective value, not as a determination that one particular preference should prevail, but simply as an indicator of subjective value, at a particular moment in time. The fact that we brush our teeth and put on clean clothes and smile at strangers and publish articles and put letters after our name simply displays to the world that we want to be respected and assigned value—either in the form of friendship, a new teaching job, or cold, hard cash, or anything else we are seeking. Do we really drive a Prius to save miles per gallon, or to *show others* how much we care about the environment or that we are wealthy enough to buy the expensive Prius? This is just like wondering if Gatsby bought his mansion because he likes big houses, or because he wants to show others he can afford big houses. Or we could wonder if he truly loves Daisy, or just wants to show that he is wealthy enough to get a girl like Daisy. Commodification is difficult for anti-capitalist critics because they feel it leads to dominance and exploitation. Austrian critics simply see it as the process of assigning value to things that are to be exchanged in order to satisfy needs or wants. And it is in the subjective assessment of value that can lead us toward another alternative economic reading of Fitzgerald's novel.

Contrary to anti-capitalist views of value, in which a good has an inherent value based upon its labor production, Austrians like Mises declare value to be completely attributed by the unique and independent preferences of individuals. "A value judgment never consists in anything other than preferring *a* to *b*," Mises explains. "It is only the market that, in establishing prices for each factor of production, creates the conditions required for economic calculation. Economic calculation always deals with prices, never with values" (*Human Action* 332). Therefore, what one perceives as value is actually just one's personal interpretation of what something is worth in relation to other market options. Goods have value simply because individuals have chosen to deem them valuable based on preferences over time. There is nothing inherently valuable about gold.

One cannot eat it for sustenance or wear it for protection. It is not stronger than other metals. And there are many resources that are rarer, so even a value premise of supply and demand is tenuous. Humans *choose* value and measure it preferentially. Gatsby's love for Daisy fits this definition of subjectivity. If we even attempt to measure her character objectively, by most accounts we would consider her to be a generally horrible person. She is superficial, deceitful, fickle, materialistic, unfaithful, unreliable, unintelligent, and careless. She is even a poor parent. However, Gatsby's subjective assessment of her is quite different and is made clear throughout the novel. Of course he admires Daisy's beauty and her wealthy upbringing, but his love is much more personal to his own character, as a business-minded investor. Nick tells us that Gatsby "found her excitingly desirable" (Fitzgerald 148), and because other men had fallen for her as well, "it increased her value in his eyes" (149). We are also told that Gatsby even used his perceived value of Daisy to assess his surroundings: "I think he revalued everything in his house according to the measure of response it drew from her well-loved eyes. Sometimes, too, he stared around at his possessions in a dazed way, as though in her actual and astounding presence none of it was any longer real" (91). This description demonstrates that subjective value not only exists, but also fluctuates.

After Gatsby's death, Nick reminds us one final time of Gatsby's overvaluation of Daisy. He concludes that Gatsby "paid a high price for living too long with a single dream. He must have looked up at an unfamiliar sky through frightening leaves and shivered as he found what a grotesque thing a rose is and how raw the sunlight was upon the scarcely created grass. A new world, material without being real" (161). Nick is describing the inherent subjectivity in assigning value, whether to a rose or to a person. Roses are, in reality, nothing more than thorny, red plants, but we assign valuable beauty to them. Similarly, Daisy is simply a vapid, idle, and spoiled young woman to whom tremendous value has been attributed by a man in pursuit of an empty dream. Her perceived value, according to Gatsby, drives every other economic action he pursues throughout the text, and it is only at the end that we discover how illusory his investment has been. As economic agents, we all choose value; it is not predetermined for us. And as Gatsby eventually learns, some things are not as valuable as we wish them to be.

We may also employ a capitalistic economic perspective to analyze one of the methods by which Gatsby obtains his wealth. It is briefly revealed that he made his fortune bootlegging during the prohibition years. The very notion of a government banning a product from the market is antithetical to Austrian economics, for two reasons. First, such an economic perspective does not believe government has the right, or the power, to control human behavior economically. Second, a government should not be allowed to pick and choose which products it deems harmful to an individual citizen. The market allows for such personal choices in which poor products will be weeded out organically through preferential human action.

While Gatsby's wealth did technically grow from breaking the law, we must remember that it was the government's intervention in the market by creating the prohibition that allowed Gatsby to become the wealthy man whom critics condemn. If alcohol were legal, Gatsby would not have been able to become so wealthy, at least not through selling liquor. A free market would have restrained his ability to achieve wealth so quickly, unless he devised a more creative enterprise. Furthermore, Austrian economics is founded upon the logic of "human action," hence the title of Ludwig von Mises's master treatise. In it, Mises writes,

> The aim of American prohibition was to prevent the individual residents of the country from drinking alcoholic beverages. But the law hypocritically did not make drinking as such illegal and did not penalize it. It merely prohibited the manufacture, the sale, and the transportation of intoxicating liquors, the business transactions which precede the act of drinking. The idea was that people indulge in the vice of drinking only because unscrupulous businessmen prevail upon them. (728)

But in the case of prohibition, businessmen didn't *create* the market of alcohol consumption; they simply satisfied it. In other words, the government regulation did not actually stop people from drinking, as it surely hoped. It simply penalized the commerce, making alcohol even more valuable for consumers and more profitable for distributors like Gatsby. Human action always supersedes government interference. Therefore, those who condemn Gatsby's wealth and subsequent behavior must also acknowledge that it was government overreach, and not true Austrian capitalism, that caused it.

Each of the aforementioned capitalistic explications is useful for very specific elements of Fitzgerald's text and its accompanying characters and plot points. However, I contend that there is a larger case to be made for economic analysis regarding the novel's premise as a whole, and it regards the representation of business cycles. In one final analysis, I would like to return to where this chapter began—the connection between the free-market economists who dissected the boom and bust period of the 1920s and the relationship between Daisy and Gatsby. First, let me borrow from Michael Tratner's essay, "A Man Is His Bonds: Deficit Spending in *The Great Gatsby*." He describes how Gatsby's behavior in the novel is reflective of the easy access to credit that boomed during the early part of the twentieth century and how spending is used as a stimulant to the rest of the economy. And it is this spending that allows Gatsby access to Daisy's life and love:

> If Daisy embodies the promise of money, Gatsby embodies immense
> desire. Indeed, Gatsby's monetary history enacts the cycle that easy
> money promised—desire that had been inhibited is released by the
> easy, almost illicit money of credit (in his case, literally illicit bonds);
> that desire released is "effective demand" or spending which then
> stimulates the whole economic system to produce licit money—sym-
> bolically, Daisy. Spending illicit money is a method of gaining access to
> the world of licit money, as spending on credit is a way of gaining an
> unmortgaged return. (368)

What must be understood first, however, and Tratner, though incomplete
in his analysis, is hinting in the right direction regarding spending, is the
functioning of the entire business cycle, as illustrated in Austrian economic theory. It is this cycle that can help us fully correlate Gatsby's
inevitable downfall with his previous trajectory with Daisy. First, let me
offer an extremely condensed explanation of the Austrian business cycle
theory. The business cycle begins with an expansion of the money supply
into an economy in which it did not previously exist. This is most often
(but not necessarily) accomplished through the printing of fiat money by
a government, which distorts the natural pricing signals of the market
through the influx of illegitimate funds. In response, banks lower interest
rates due to the increase in the money supply, which then stimulates
borrowing. This increased borrowing leads to increased spending toward
investments that are less reliable than other available options. Therefore,
the misallocation of resources causes malinvestments that ultimately will
not come to fruition in the form of successful profit. The market, fooled
by inaccurate pricing signals, cannot support these investments for long.
A credit crunch results in which banks cease lending in order to protect
real capital. This causes production to stop, which causes deeper debt.
Ultimately, an economic depression ensues, which is the only way for the
market to readjust itself toward more legitimate uses of funds (Ebeling).
It is this theory that perfectly explains the boom and bust of the 1920s
economy and metaphorically mirrors the rise and fall of Gatsby's relationship with Daisy.

The cycle begins through the process of introducing new and illicit
money into the system. We already know that Gatsby represents the
nouveau riche of the time, so his wealth provides a point of conflict with
the established, East Coast blue-bloods. And the confusion over where
Gatsby's wealth has come from indicates the façade of stability that
undergirds Gatsby's own life, as well as a real-world economy. In chapter
4, Gatsby tells Nick that he inherited "a good deal of money" as "the son
of some wealthy people in the Middle West—all dead now" (Fitzgerald
60). Then, in chapter 5, Gatsby claims to have earned his wealth in a span
of three years. When Nick questions his inheritance, Gatsby deflects by
saying that he lost most of it during the war, and explains that he invested in a variety of businesses, including drug stores and oil (90). By

chapter 7 we are made aware that Tom has investigated Gatsby and revealed some of the illegal activities that have produced Gatsby's wealth (133). Each of the versions of Gatsby's story is clouded in mystery, as if his money simply appeared, depending on which rumor one happened to hear. Gatsby himself even seems to produce magically signs of money and influence at a moment's notice out of thin air—medals, a card from the commissioner, fancy shirts. In fact, the famous shirts themselves, as they are carelessly flung from the cabinet, seem to represent new currency, boldly stamped out by an enchanted printing press and presenting an abundant source of superficial prosperity. Nick describes for us "his shirts, piled like bricks in stacks a dozen high. . . . He took out a pile of shirts and began throwing them, one by one, before us. . . . While we admired he brought more" (92). The symbol of money without the backing of a legitimate currency standard that everyone can easily recognize is the beginning of an economic system's downfall.

But it is Gatsby's business connections that serve the defining role of illicit money in the novel, whereby we gather through several clues (particularly at the end when Nick answers a secretive phone call intended for Gatsby) that Gatsby has made at least some of his vast fortune peddling forged or illegitimate bonds. This model fits with the real-world economic function of bonds, as the government has always been a primary promoter of bond issues, selling a long term investment at a reasonable present rate of purchase. This was especially true during Fitzgerald's time, as government bonds were commonplace during the war. Through this, the government (or whatever entity is issuing the bond) goes, in effect, into debt in the short term so as to repay the yield over time. By participating in a fake bond scheme, Gatsby is aiding his associates in the production of fiat money, funds which are not backed by any legitimately stable form of currency. By amassing wealth that is founded upon false money, the market Gatsby inhabits, his Long Island environment of traditional East Coast elites, becomes distorted and more accessible than it otherwise would have been. It is this access that has allowed Gatsby the opportunity to reconnect with Daisy.

In the economic analogy that I am offering here, Daisy's past represents an established banking system, one which indicates a wealthy past founded upon legitimate reserves and steady investments. Contrary to Tratner's analysis, it is not the bonds that extend credit, it is the banks. Money alone does not allow access to the prestige of historic wealth; it must be granted by those existing in it. It is only Daisy, and blue-blooded people like her, who can grant access to the East Egg lifestyle and comfortable future so desperately desired by middle-class individuals and the newly rich, dispensing credit to those who want to participate in it and appear to be worthy of fitting in. Adding to the bank comparison, it is well documented that Daisy (and her environment) is described throughout the novel with words like "silver," "gold," "green," and "money," further signifying that she exists in a world governed by monetary policy, the embodiment of financial exchange. With Gatsby's background of shady financial deals and Daisy's background of stable wealth eventually coinciding, the characters themselves then become part of the trade process. Gatsby attempts to engage his illicit funds as a means for accessing the world of authentic money. As Tratner cleverly puns, Gatsby is "trying to move from illegitimate to legitimate bonds" (367). He seeks to invest in Daisy's love, the ultimate business venture that he hopes offers consistent financial returns and long-lasting emotional happiness.

Gatsby's past as a poor student and soldier, however, once reflected a high interest rate on Daisy's love. Without the confidence that Gatsby would be able to provide the life Daisy demands, Gatsby was unable to access her love, and consequently, her world. We see this failed extension of credit during the flashback to five years prior, as Gatsby's attempted investment in her love was unsuccessful:

> He took what he could get, ravenously and unscrupulously—eventually he took Daisy on a still October night, took her because he had no real right to touch her hand. He might have despised himself, for he had certainly taken her under false pretenses. I don't mean that he had traded on his phantom millions, but he had deliberately given Daisy a sense of security; he let her believe that he was a person from much the same stratum as herself—that he was fully able to take care of her. As a matter of fact, he had no such facilities—he had no comfortable family standing behind him, and he was liable at the whim of an impersonal government to be blown anywhere about the world. (Fitzgerald 149)

Gatsby's attempt to infiltrate Daisy's world resembles an anxious home-buyer trying to fill out a loan application on a house she knows she could never afford, but takes pleasure in simply signing the hopeful documents. Gatsby hung on to this hope for as long as could, during their romantic encounter years before, hoping he had disguised himself well enough to convince Daisy that he was worthy. But Daisy wanted to invest in tangible things, not hopes for the future or dreams of magical love. She desired clarity and immediacy, which was instead fulfilled by Tom: "There was a wholesome bulkiness about his person and his position, and Daisy was flattered" (151). Tom was safe and stable, at least financially and socially speaking, thus her credit and access to her world was extended to him, rather than to the uncertainty of Gatsby. However, now that Gatsby presents himself as having plenty of money, the interest rate begins to fall precipitously, as he now appears more capable of repaying Daisy's risk of loving him back through financial stability. The Austrian business cycle is now underway, as Mises explains:

> A drop in the gross market rate of interest affects the entrepreneur's calculation concerning the chances of the profitability of projects considered. . . . The result of this calculation shows the businessman

whether or not a definite project will pay. It shows him what investments can be made under the given state of the ratio in the public's
valuation of future goods as against present goods. It brings his actions
into agreement with this valuation. (*Human Action* 550)

Gatsby is now in a position to engage in an investment for which before
he was not qualified. He is able to calculate his odds of success in attaining her love and his active pursuit of her begins. But his calculation on
her return is based on misleading information, which can have disastrous
consequences. These calculations, Mises writes, "make projects appear
profitable and realizable which a correct calculation, based on an interest
rate not manipulated by credit expansion, would have shown as unreal-
izable. Entrepreneurs embark upon an execution of such projects. Business activities are stimulated. A boom begins" (550).

Before actively pursuing Daisy, however, Gatsby becomes known in
the novel by the exorbitant parties he hosts, representing the lavish
spending during the prosperous 1920s. Gatsby's opulent gatherings, and
his pursuit of Daisy, are expensive investments through which he hopes
that the community and Daisy will then invest more in him. "Gatsby's
parties represent a general willingness to spend money that is stimulated
and created by the 'promise of money,'" Tratner writes. "People will
spend if they believe that they can attract the kind of money that had
seemed reserved for the rich" (368). Gatsby's spending allows his consumers to "buy" status and enjoyment by being seen at his luxurious parties. Likewise, his spending is an attempt to entice Daisy to "buy into" his
new persona with hopes of a new and loving future. Daisy and his party
guests are potential consumers that will use Gatsby's funds for their own
status and enjoyment, as well as to reinvest in him. We witness the extent
of overspending when a number of Gatsby's guests are said to have
never even been invited in the first place: "Lots of people come who
haven't been invited," [Daisy] said suddenly. "That girl hadn't been invited. They simply force their way in and he's too polite to object" (Fitzgerald 108). Much like a person being given a cheap loan from a bank
without truly qualifying for it or even asking for it, this "free money" is
malinvested because the chance at repayment is reduced. Again, money
lent without repercussions or returns leads to a false prosperity that must
come to an end.

This malinvestment appears to work, though, for much of the novel as
guests are always happy, Gatsby's reputation grows, and Daisy begins to
fall for him once again. He is fitting in to the elite crowd, as credit continues to be extended in the form of "Gatsby's notoriety, spread about by
the hundreds who had accepted his hospitality" (Fitzgerald 97). The
more credit Daisy (and everyone else in the environment of established
wealth) releases, through signs that she is interested in him and through
increased access to her world, the more Gatsby invests, the more parties

he throws and the more he pursues Daisy. She is instantly excited at finally attending a Gatsby party, telling Nick (through monetary descriptions) that she is "giving out green," and offering a "gold pencil" to write down names and addresses (104–5). She is acting like she wants to invest in Gatsby's new market. But Tom doesn't know anyone there, saying, "We don't go around very much." This implies that he is much more careful with his money (credit), only spending on things he can tangibly use. Though she believes the crowd to be "more interesting than the people we know" (108), Daisy quickly becomes hardened in the presence of the emptiness of the people of West Egg. She believes its residents are simply following "a short-cut from nothing to nothing," that they are commoners and will never garner the prestige of the truly wealthy and powerful (107). Daisy ultimately recognizes that she does not fit in with West Egg culture. In an effort to avoid East Egg gossip and to appease Daisy, Gatsby begins cutting back on the parties, and even fires most of his employees (114), because he must divert funding from one sector of investments (perhaps one that was actually more productive) in order to sustain his expensive investment in Daisy's love. He must save in order to protect capital. His investment strategy seems to pay off, as Daisy soon kisses Gatsby and tell him she loves him (116). Mises echoes the effects of this investment:

> Some of the investments made in the boom period . . . must simply be abandoned because the current means required for their further exploitation cannot be recovered; this "circulating" capital is more urgently needed in other branches of want-satisfaction; the proof is that it can be employed in a more profitable way in other fields." (*Human Action* 561)

But we soon recognize that Gatsby's investment in Daisy's love is potentially too large, his hopes too high. While touring Gatsby's mansion with Daisy, Nick wonders, "There must have been moments even that afternoon when Daisy tumbled short his dreams—not through her own fault, but because of the colossal vitality of his illusion" (Fitzgerald 95). Gatsby is practically blinded by his faith in her reciprocation, his return on investment. As the cycle demonstrates, increased credit provides opportunities for misplaced investments. Gatsby overvalues Daisy's love and invests too much in her. She is not everything he thinks she is or remembers her to be. In the end, Gatsby continues his expensive investment by offering to take the blame for Daisy's murderous driving (Fitzgerald 143).

Though Gatsby's relationship is on the brink of destruction, Nick says, "He couldn't possibly leave Daisy until he knew what she was going to do. He was clutching at some last hope and I couldn't bear to shake him free" (Fitzgerald 148). Even in Nick's final conversation with Gatsby, we see him assuming Daisy will call and seeking Nick's affirmation (154). Gatsby cannot bear to face his new future. Mises confirms this behavior in those that have lost their ability to access credit, believing they still possess the avenue to affluence: "The process of readjustment, even in the absence of any new credit expansion, is delayed by the psychological effects of disappointment and frustration. People are slow to free themselves from the self-deception of delusive prosperity" (*Human Action* 576). And we wonder if they will eventually repeat their foolish actions in future cycles.

When deciding what to do in the oppressive heat, Daisy wonders what will come of them in the next thirty years. Jordan says, "Life starts all over again when it gets crisp in the fall" (Fitzgerald 118), and we know that the season arrives near the conclusion of the novel with the arrival of "an autumn flavor in the air" (153). We assume that these people will continue living tumultuous lives, riding booms and busts because of malinvestments. After all, people like Daisy (and the wealthy institution she represents) are ultimately "bailed out" by not facing the consequences of their actions. Money shields Tom and Daisy from responsibility, and Nick's anger at this result is clearly evident in the final pages: "They were careless people, Tom and Daisy—they smashed up things and creatures and then retreated back into their money or their vast carelessness, or whatever it was that kept them together, and let other people clean up the mess they had made" (179). Like a bank that gives out risky loans and runs out of money, Daisy is bailed out by the accommodating environment, causing tragic ripples throughout larger economic systems. George and Myrtle, representative of the common citizen and working class, bear the brunt of Gatsby and Daisy's actions: "The immense majority," Mises writes, "must foot the bill for the malinvestments and the overconsumption of the boom episode" (*Human Action* 562). In this case, Daisy's inability or unwillingness to continue her fiscal relationship with Gatsby, opting instead for the reliability of Tom, causes a crash, a realignment of spending priorities. Gatsby must reconsider where he spends his future. "As soon as the afflux of additional fiduciary media comes to an end," Mises writes, "the airy castle of the boom collapses. The entrepreneurs must restrict their activities because they lack the funds for their continuation on the exaggerated scale" (560).

Due to the ultimate failure of his investment in Daisy's love, Gatsby must realign his spending priorities, taking advantage of opportunities he ignored previously. Rather than trying to impress his neighbors and woo Daisy on a nightly basis, we see him finally desire to take a swim in his luxurious pool that he had neglected. He tells Nick, "You know, old sport, I've never used that pool all summer?" (Fitzgerald 153). Though it is a simple pleasure, it is a cheap and available respite from depressive conditions. Certain economic actions are now possible for investors in the wake of the faltering misplaced investments: "They can find partial compensation and the fact that some enjoyments are now available to them" now that the "*orgies* of the boom" have subsided, Mises explains. "It is slight compensation only, as their demand for those other things which they do not get because of inappropriate employment of capital goods is more intense than their demand for these 'substitutes,' as it were. But it is the only choice left of them as conditions and data are now" (*Human Action* 561). We are able to see a linguistic similarity between Mises and Fitzgerald in the famous last lines of the novel: "Gatsby believed in the green light, the orgastic future that year by year receded before us" (Fitzgerald 180). The words *orgiastic* and *orgastic*, famously, have been interchanged depending on the particular edition of Fitzgerald's novel. This link in language highlights for us Gatsby's extravagant and romantic vision and its inevitable juxtaposition with realistic economic conditions. No matter what economic agency one imagines, he must continually be aware of the competing choices available for his economic action.

In Nick Carraway's opening descriptions of Gatsby, he is identified as an "extraordinary gift for hope" (2). Gatsby embodies the potential for rebirth and a reimagining of what is possible. However, Gatsby's hope (or everyone else's hope in him) is inextricably linked to the past. Perhaps Gatsby's greatest downfall, from a business perspective, is his infatuation with the past and inability to project a clear and stable future. Austrian School economist Murray Rothbard writes,

> The entrepreneurial function is the function of forecasting the uncertain future. Before embarking on any investment or line of production, the entrepreneur, or "enterpriser," must estimate present and future costs and future revenues and therefore estimate whether and how much profits he will earn from the investment. If he forecasts well and significantly better than his business competitors, he will reap profits from his investment. The better his forecasting, the higher the profits he will earn. If, on the other hand, he is a poor forecaster and overestimates the demand for his product, he will suffer losses and pretty soon be forced out of the business. ("Economic Depressions" 71)

Throughout the novel, we can see that Gatsby is attempting to amend his previously failed relationship with Daisy, one that existed when he was a very different person. Gatsby's redemptive vision is illustrated most clearly when Nick daringly tells Gatsby, "You can't repeat the past." Gatsby answers, "Why of course you can!" . . . "I'm going to fix everything just the way it was before. . . . She'll see" (110). However, an entrepreneur who makes investments in an attempt to recreate previous conditions is likely doomed to fail. Success is found in understanding the future, not reliving the past. Mises writes,

> Entrepreneurs often err. They pay heavily for their errors. . . . What distinguishes the successful entrepreneur and promoter from other people is precisely the fact that he does not let himself be guided by what was and is, but arranges his affairs on the ground of his opinion about the future. He sees the past and the present as other people do; but he judges the future in a different way. In his actions he is directed

by an opinion about the future which deviates from those held by the crowd. (582)

A successful investor must relinquish the past and forge ahead to new possibilities. It is not Gatsby's pursuit of a former love that defeats him; rather, it is Gatsby's assumption that the market still exists under previous conditions and his neglect of future circumstances which entices his poor investment in an unreciprocated love that ultimately fails him.

To summarize, from an Austrian economic perspective, Gatsby's wealth is representative of the influx of new and illegitimate money into a market, and Daisy, under the illusion that his wealth is real, expands credit to him just as a bank or government entity might. With a massive infusion of spending, and a subsequent failure (or crash), Gatsby's trajectory offers, in Austrian terms, a "boom and bust cycle" of over-extended credit. This process, expertly defined by Ludwig von Mises and Friedrich Hayek, who won the Nobel Prize in economics for his business cycle theory, emphasizes the false relationship between monetary spending and real investment. Without adequate returns or demands, overspending creates an inflation that cannot be sustained and must fail in an attempt to reach a measure of market equilibrium. Gatsby's enormous spending to achieve not only acceptance in his Long Island community, but to gain Daisy's love, especially since it is ultimately left unfulfilled, demands a crash in order to return stability to the market environment.

Many people's beliefs about business cycles are based upon preconceived notions regarding the dangerous instability of capitalism. These ideas are founded in anti-capitalist doctrine. Karl Marx determined that before the Industrial Revolution, economic systems tended to find a moderately consistent equilibrium, with virtually no wild swings in growth or reduction, no booms or busts (McLellan 543–44). Rothbard explains that because of the apparent chronological connection between emerging business cycles and modern industry, Marx surmised that capitalism causes such market swings. Therefore, the capitalistic, free-market economy must be responsible for such hazardous volatility (69). Rather, as Austrian theorists have come to know, it is the introduction of illegitimate and unsustainable money (often by way of the government printing press, but in Gatsby's case, through the forging of bonds) into a system that inflates currency and harmfully influences interest rates that causes tumultuous swings in economic activity, resulting in booms and busts. By condemning capitalism, more authority has been given to government to quell economic fluctuations, and more spending among the public, not just the wealthy, has been urged as a means of maintaining equilibrium. This perspective not only evolved in the minds of the public, but in the minds of economic thinkers as well. John Maynard Keynes, according to Tratner, wrote that "the growth of wealth, so far from being dependent upon the abstinence of the rich, as is commonly supposed, is more likely to be impeded by it." What economists like Keynes concluded was that money spent by the rich was simply not enough to sustain an economy. More spending by everyone was needed. "The desires of the masses had to be released as well," Tratner writes (368). Thus, with Keynes's help, America began expensive public works and redistribution programs in order to get money to the masses to spend. However, this plan is also ultimately doomed to fail.

Contrary to popular belief, capitalism is based on *saving*, not spending. Delayed gratification and postponed consumption allows for true investment in a legitimate future. As Mises writes, "Saving is the first step on the way toward improvement of material well-being and toward every further progress on this way" (487). While Austrian economics certainly promotes the freedom to spend one's money however one wishes, the frivolity of emotional goals and short-term gains is not the path of the classical Austrian capitalist. Even love ultimately isn't worth the expense for Gatsby. What we discover through this new kind of critical reading is that Gatsby is practicing, as is the philandering Tom, both in the smaller economy of their social circles, the same spending habits that anti-free market, government interventionist policies often embrace. This inevitably leads to a tremendous crash, which is seen in the real world at the end of the 1920s, and in Gatsby's fictional world at the tragic end of the novel. As Mises presciently notes, "Depression is the aftermath of credit expansion" (*Planning for Freedom* 7).

We can learn a great deal about business activity through examining the relationship between Gatsby and Daisy. Early in the novel, Jordan Baker ominously states, "It takes two to make an accident" (58). This is often viewed as illustrating the frivolity of the wealthy class, mindlessly spending for the sake of unfulfilled promises, shallow appearances, or pursuing dreams that lay waste to those around them. Viewed through the lens of Austrian economics, however, suddenly the characters of Gatsby and Daisy are slightly altered, as are the social dynamics (both in the fiction and in the reality of the 1920s) we have always observed. These characters are now economic agents, responding to signals around them, as we all do. We may not respect their human qualities of selfishness or superficiality, but we gain a new understanding of how mistakes can be made based on economic perceptions of a marketplace that is constantly changing. Gatsby and Daisy (as well as Tom, Jordan, Nick, and others) are not despicable because they have money. They simply act, as every human does, in their interests, and are susceptible to making poor decisions because of false market indicators. By simultaneously overvaluing each other, Gatsby and Daisy create the consequential accident to which Jordan refers. And they must pay the consequences for their economic decisions, which Gatsby does, as this is the only way to restore a sense of equilibrium to the market. Rather than defaulting to traditional anti-capitalist interpretations of power dynamics, wealth disparity, and commodification, Fitzgerald's text is brought to new life for both previous and emerging audiences with an Austrian capitalist reading. We may gain a further understanding of economic systems, as well as the humans that affect them and are affected by them, through their myriad individual choices. This is the benefit of questioning familiar anticapitalist critical approaches and exploring a new methodology of literary study by way of Austrian economics.

FOUR

"The Monster's Sick"

Rural Economics in The Grapes of Wrath

Early in John Steinbeck's *The Grapes of Wrath*, the Joad family members, facing eviction from the land they work as tenant farmers, blame banks for taking over the land they had spent so long working and bemoan the development of massive tractors that begin to replace human farmers. We sympathize with them as we understand their attachment to the land, their tireless work ethic, and their familial bonds that have evolved over generations. And we wonder if the life that the Joads, and so many other farmers of the 1930s, had made could have been salvaged and encouraged to prosper once again. In this chapter, I will primarily focus on the economic and historical reality behind the removal of tenant farmers during the 1930s and the involvement of the United States government in the agriculture industry. Economic history shows us that banks of the time did not instantly become greedy and cruel landowners intent on ruining the lives of innocent farmers. Rather, it is more accurate to say they were following incentives put in place by the federal government. Steinbeck's novel offers an economic reading which clearly exemplifies how the Austrian economic perspective is not aligned with any particular political party. An economist of the Austrian school would argue that the market interventionism of Republican president Herbert Hoover led the United States into the Great Depression and Democratic president Franklin Roosevelt's policies later worsened it.

In chapter 5 of the novel, Steinbeck offers a passage in a stream-of-consciousness style that parallels the exasperated tone of the farmers he represents and seems to presage much of the economic literary criticism that has emerged regarding *The Grapes of Wrath*:

> If a bank or a finance company owned the land, the owner man said, the bank—or the Company—needs—wants—insists—must have—as though the Bank or the Company were a monster, with thought and feeling, which had ensnared them. These last would take no responsibility for the banks or the companies because they were men and slaves, while the banks were machines and Masters all at the same time . . .

> But—you see, a bank or a company can do that, because those creatures don't breathe air, don't eat side-meat. They breathe profits; they eat the interest on money. If they don't get it, they die the way you die without air, without side-meat. It is a sad thing, but it is so. It is just so. . . .

> And at last the owner men came to a point. The tenant system won't work anymore. One man on a tractor can take the place of 12 or 14 families. Pay him a wage and take all the crap. We have to do it. We don't like to do it. But the monster's sick. Something's happened to the monster.

> But you'll kill the land with cotton. We know. We've got to take cotton quick before the land dies. Then we'll sell the land. . . .

> The bank is something more than men, I tell you. It's the monster. Men made it, but they can't control it. (41–43)

A traditional anti-capitalist reading of the novel highlights the faceless corporate behemoth that oppresses the Joads. The banks are inhumane and ruthless as they seek profits at any cost, ignoring the personal and laborious efforts of the men, women, and children that actually developed the land that has allowed the banks to prosper. Nellie Y. McKay writes, "*The Grapes of Wrath* delineates the tragedy of an agrarian family in a world in which capitalist greed and the demands of rapidly advancing technology supersede human needs and extenuating financial circumstances" (101). David N. Cassuto narrows this larger anti-capitalist theme down to the fetishistic relationship with natural resources inherent in capitalism. He writes that since land and water are necessary to human survival, they become commodified, as "any item of exchange value acquires symbolic value, connoting power and wealth and thereby enhancing the prestige of its possessor" (133). As the Joads lose this authority over their resources, they subsequently lose power in their own personal and cultural existence. The novel's portrayal of class stratification is defined by the control of natural resources. The Joads, and farmers like them, "have become components of the factory-farming process," Cassuto writes, "economically distant from their bourgeois oppressors but closely tied to the industrial ethos that rewards the subjugation of nature" (133).

This reading echoes Steinbeck's own economic concerns, which he related in his journalistic work *The Harvest Gypsies*, a collection of essays he produced on his travels studying migrant agricultural labor in preparation for writing *The Grapes of Wrath*. He felt for the migrants because the Oklahomans "are not migrants by nature. They are gypsies by force of circumstances" (22). Steinbeck was greatly concerned when one large farm owner reportedly told him that "the success of California agriculture requires that we create and maintain a peon class" (23). Traditional anti-capitalist criticism embraces the proletariat in its conflict with the bourgeoisie, attempting to amend those circumstances that have promoted injustice and debased humanity. In his 1939 review of the novel for the Marxist publication *New Masses*, critic Granville Hicks said the novel "has all the qualities proletarian literature has to have" (139). He admired Steinbeck's economic presentation in the novel, as "his insight into capitalism illuminates every chapter of the book. . . . Steinbeck knows both how things happen and why they happen, and he shows the why working itself out in the how" (141). "No writer of our times," Hicks continued, "has a more acute sense of economic forces, and of the way they operate against the interests of the masses of the people" (142). During his research in preparing to write the novel, Steinbeck wrote in a letter, "I want to put a tag of shame on the greedy bastards who are responsible for this" (*A Life in Letters* 162). Clearly, Steinbeck was voicing his frustrations with the banks and landowners, the representations of outsized agribusiness, and aiming at defending poverty-stricken farmers and migrants in the larger battle between the anti-capitalist definitions of bourgeoisie and proletariat. And, by many accounts, Steinbeck was immensely successful in his revolutionary vision. Journalist Herbert Agar wrote at the time, "The book is so true that in addition to being great art it is great sociology" (qtd. in "Red Meat and Red Herrings" 72). But while the novel's sociology may be considered great, it is its economics and history that must be brought into question here, along with Steinbeck's economic understanding of the how and why of what the Joads were experiencing.

There are a number of reasons why the Great Depression was more severe than the many other economic recessions our nation had previously endured—among them the manipulation of the gold standard; massive tax increases; unwise credit expansion; heavy import/export tariffs—and this was on top of the drought that began in 1930 and the dust storms that decimated farms across the American plains throughout the middle of the decade. For this examination of *The Grapes of Wrath*, however, I will only focus on one particularly catastrophic cause of agricultural and economic failure in Steinbeck's novel of the 1930s: government intervention into the free market. Government meddling in the business of farming was not only the primary cause of the Joads' struggles, but it prolonged those struggles, and those of millions of Americans just like them, far beyond what had been previously experienced in down economies. I will try to demonstrate that corporate finance was not the primary enemy of the Joads, and perhaps it was the federal government that behaved most monstrously of all.

One of the larger misperceptions of twentieth century American history is that Republican president Herbert Hoover was a proponent of laissez-faire economics, and that it was the promotion of capitalist policies under his leadership that caused the Great Depression. To the contrary, Hoover was a hyper-interventionist whose interference with the U.S. economy harmed farmers like the Joads in countless ways. Progressive economic policies of the early twentieth century were losing steam by the time Hoover became a political leader. His reinvigoration of intense government planning is what led the way for our nation's most interventionist president, Franklin D. Roosevelt, who actually followed in Hoover's footsteps. Even Roosevelt's economic adviser, Rexford Tugwell, said the implementation of the far-reaching New Deal policies "owed much to Hoover" (DiLorenzo 160). Earlier, when Hoover became secretary of commerce in 1921, he stated his ultimate goal was "the transformation of American society," and he "believed that human manipulation could triumph over any alleged 'laws' of economics" (161). In order to achieve these lofty goals, Hoover moved to increase the commerce department's budget by over 50 percent and added over 3,000 government officials in thirty new divisions (161). His extensive efforts to produce American wealth by way of centralized planning are the exact opposite of laissez-faire economics and completely antithetical to the Austrian School of economic policy.

Through massive farm subsidies and price-support programs over the course of the 1920s, also endorsed by Republican presidents Calvin Coolidge and Warren G. Harding, Hoover funneled billions of dollars to federal spending for farmers in an attempt to appease the growing agricultural lobby. Throughout the decade, countless bureaucratic agencies developed, often as a result of trying to cure a problem that was caused by a previous bureaucratic agency. Ultimately, the Federal Farm Board, established in 1929 by newly-elected President Hoover, was perhaps the primary culprit for the farmers' problems during the Depression. With $500 million from the U.S. Treasury at its disposal, the Federal Farm Board doled out loans to farm co-ops (groups of farmers working together) at low interest rates and founded a stabilization organization to support crop prices and curb surpluses. However, Hoover appointed to the Board men who were chosen by the co-ops and had vested interests in maintaining government subsidies. This resulted in an enormous agricultural cartel—enacted by the Hoover administration, supported by the coercive power of the federal government, and guided by and for the members of the cartel themselves (Rothbard 227–28).

Furthermore, Hoover chose two of America's most economically and politically important crops, wheat and cotton, and mandated minimum pricing for them. This means that the United States government would *guarantee* prices for these respective crops. In an attempt to shield two major farming constituencies from declining market prices, Hoover only exacerbated the economic imbalance in production. Since prices were now guaranteed, cotton and wheat farmers began to grow as much as possible, either through expanding their acreage or by discarding other crops in favor of guaranteed ones. The result? In only two years of massive overproduction, the Federal Farm Board spent $500 million on price subsidies; ended up shutting down the reimbursement program as a failure; and either gave away or sold at massive losses millions upon millions of units of wheat and cotton (Folsom 61–62). Esteemed economist Murray Rothbard, in discussing Hoover's foolish cartel schemes from an Austrian perspective, roundly condemns such government policies:

> The grandiose stabilization effort of the FFB failed ignominiously. Its loans encouraged greater production, adding to its farm surpluses, which overhung the market, driving prices down. . . . The FFB thus aggravated the very farm depression that it was supposed to solve. With the FFB generally acknowledged a failure, President Hoover began to pursue the inexorable logic of government intervention to the next step: recommending that productive land be withdrawn from cultivation, that crops be plowed under, and that immature farm animals be slaughtered—all to reduce the very surpluses that government's prior intervention had brought into being. (234)

Thus, Steinbeck's vivid depiction of the Joads' plight is missing some important historical context that may mislead some of his readers who have not taken into account the fuller economic circumstances of the time.

In perhaps the most beautifully written section of *The Grapes of Wrath*, chapter 25, Steinbeck poetically describes the horrific reality of the subsequent stage of government intervention into the business of agriculture:

> The works of the roots of the vines, of the trees, must be destroyed to keep up the price, and this is the saddest, bitterest thing of all. Carloads of oranges dumped on the ground. The people came from miles to take the fruit, but this could not be. How would they buy oranges at twenty cents a dozen if they could drive out and pick them up? And men with hoses squirt kerosene on the oranges, and they are angry at the crime, angry at the people who come to take the fruit. A million people hungry, needing the fruit—and kerosene sprayed over the golden mountains. . . .

> Dump potatoes in the rivers and place guards along the banks to keep the hungry people from fishing them out. Slaughter the pigs and bury them, and let the putrescence trip down into the earth. . . .

> And children dying of pellagra must die because a profit cannot be taken from an orange. And coroners must fill in the certificates—died of malnutrition—because the food must rot, must be forced to rot.

The people come with nets to fish for potatoes in the river, and the
guards hold them back; they come in rattling cars to get the dumped
oranges, but the kerosene sprayed. And they stand still and watched
potatoes flow by, listen to the screaming pigs being killed in a ditch
and covered with quicklime, watch the mountains of oranges slop
down to a putrefying ooze; and in the eyes of the people there is the
failure; and in the eyes of the hungry there is a growing wrath. (448–49)

This wrath is understandable for the Joads and other farmers of the time.
However, if they more clearly understood where they could have directed that anger, perhaps a different understanding of the novel could
emerge.

Historian John Flynn writes that prior to his election as president,
"Roosevelt had told the voters they would see no cruel jokes like plowing
up cotton or not planting wheat or buying up crops to raise prices, all of
which had been urged on farmers" under the Hoover administration (48).
Of course, what actually happened was that Roosevelt and his bureaucrats killed millions of hogs, scorched fields of oats, and plowed under
cotton, all while, in a cruelly ironic twist, "the Department of Agriculture
issued a bulletin telling the nation that the great problem of our time was
our failure to produce enough food to provide the people with a mere
subsistence diet" (48). Historian Jim Powell reminds us how government
policies that allowed California peaches to rot in orchards and six million
pigs to be slaughtered "was just the sort of thing that John Steinbeck
protested against in his 1939 novel *The Grapes of Wrath*" (134). If only
Steinbeck had better known toward whom to vent his frustrations. As we
now know, Steinbeck should have been angered not with banks or landowners, but with his own federal government.

When Franklin D. Roosevelt was elected president in 1932, his new
government program, the Agricultural Adjustment Act (AAA), continued the Hoover administration's faulty interventionism by again paying
farmers to destroy land and livestock or not to produce in the first place.
Again, in an effort to assist farmers by artificially keeping prices higher
than the supply warranted, the government's involvement worsened the
Depression. In summary, this is what the AAA did: "first, some farmers
would be paid not to produce on part of their land; second, farm prices
would be pegged to the purchasing power of farm prices in 1910; third,
millers and processors would pay for much of the cost of the program.
What's more, power would be centralized to the secretary of agriculture,
who would set the processing taxes, target the price of many commod-
ities, and tell farmers how much land to remove" (Folsom 60). This misguided set of policies resulted in exactly what the Joads were facing.

Moreover, Roosevelt's plan for massive government intervention into
agriculture was not intended to be a short-term, disaster-oriented fix, but
rather a long-term economic policy: "It was their intention — as it is mine
[Roosevelt's] — to pass from the purely emergency phases necessitated by

a grave national crisis to a longtime, more permanent plan for American agriculture" (qtd. in Folsom 64–65). Of course, this meant an enormous increase in government bureaucracy, with the Department of Agriculture employing over 100,000 men (all paid through taxpayer funding) to assess the appropriate amount of land each farmer would be allowed to work. Though the AAA deemed that farmers could refuse to participate in the paid-not-to-plant scheme, most soon realized they could make more money being funded by the government instead of working their land. This misguided incentive program ultimately allowed farmers to set aside and get paid for their worst sections of land, or land they never intended to plant on anyway. They could then use the taxpayer funding to buy fertilizer for the land they did use, which led to over-farming, product surplus (again), and the deterioration of good soil. We must remember that all of this was going on during the highest periods of unemployment and poverty in our nation's history. One radio commentator, and a supporter of the Roosevelt administration, ultimately realized the complicated and disastrous nature of government involvement in agriculture:

> As soon as the AAA helped one group of farmers, other groups were affected and called for similar benefits and protective regulations. If one particular crop was controlled, the farmer would plant excessively in other crops. If acreage was controlled, he would use only his best acres. That produced a new surplus, which also had to be controlled. Farmers were paid millions of dollars *not* to produce crops while Pres. Roosevelt was telling us that one third of our people were ill fed. For every problem that was solved two or three new problems were created. (qtd. in Folsom 66)

Adding further irony to an already sadly ironic historical account, political manipulation of the price of food did help some farmers, but it came at the expense of those who needed food the most. After the implementation of the AAA policies, food and clothing prices jumped. People already hurt by the Depression now had an even harder time obtaining nourishment and clothing. With spending on these items down, businesses had to lay off workers, which of course led to more unemployment (Folsom 67). Not only were we not able to feed our own citizens because of crop and livestock reduction, but national debt continued to increase because we began to import the very items we were destroying. The United States, perhaps the most resource-rich nation on the planet, began importing oats after burning its own, lard after killing its own pigs, and corn after cutting corn production (Flynn 49). Economist Thomas J. DiLorenzo summarizes the government failures this way:

> FDR adopted a program of paying farmers millions of dollars annually for literally burning their crops and slaughtering their livestock while many Americans were going hungry. . . . This policy of reducing food

production when many Americans were going hungry created a public relations disaster for Roosevelt, who then wised up and began paying farmers and ranchers *for not raising livestock and planting crops in the first place* [italics in original]. The AAA . . . was an awful burden on poor sharecroppers, thousands of whom were evicted so that the landowners could collect their governmental bounties for not producing. Who needs sharecroppers when being paid not to grow crops? (189–90)

Without a free-market pricing system, as Austrian economists advocate, real information of supply and demand cannot be disseminated throughout the market. As we can see from the political intervention from both parties, this tampering with the market causes a devastating cycle that ultimately harms producers and consumers alike.

The final segment of *The Grapes of Wrath* that must be mentioned regarding federal intervention into the lives of poor farmers like the Joads pertains to the government camps that emerged as part of the relief efforts of New Deal policies. In the novel, Steinbeck describes Weedpatch Camp as almost utopian. With running water, stable shelter, low rent, and a self-governed community of migrants, the government-funded Weedpatch Camp appears to be the idyllic answer to economic hardship. Various social and educational activities like Saturday night dances and schooling for children take place. The camp appears to give the laborers a sense of security and dignity so they can comfortably resume their search for work—a legitimate resting place on the return road to self-sufficiency. However, some economic questions are never answered in Steinbeck's novel. We are left wondering where the money to pay for these camps comes from, knowing that any investment through federal taxation is simply reappropriated money that could have been invested elsewhere, such as in a long-term industry endeavor that could have provided consistent employment for needy workers. We also witness that the Joads are not able to stay at the camp for long, because there is no employment to be had—perhaps because all the money is going to water and tents and not to productive employment. We must also ask what Jim Rawley, the camp manager, actually does for his salary, since it appears the responsible and hard-working migrants take care of everything in the camp: "The people here worked me out of a job," Rawley says. "They keep the camp clean, they keep order, they do everything" (Steinbeck, *The Grapes of Wrath* 390–91). So what exactly are taxpayers paying him for? We wonder lastly if other government camps were as effective in comforting migrants as Weedpatch appeared to be. It is this final point that we shall investigate here.

Brian Q. Cannon writes that Steinbeck's portrayal of government camps was far from ideal: "Low wages and sporadic employment, the derision of outsiders, camp rules, a lack of privacy, and scant protection from the elements made life in a federal farm workers' camp more difficult than it appeared in *The Grapes of Wrath*" (19). Some of the camps certainly offered respite from the extreme poverty, hunger, and illness that plagued the migrant laborers, and for many, spirits were raised and new opportunities were offered. But for others, government camps were actually considered a step down in living conditions, even among those hardest hit Dust Bowl travelers. In the novel, upon arriving at Weed-patch, Tom looks admiringly across the camp "between the rows of tents," seeing that "the rows were straight and that there was no litter about the tents" (Steinbeck 370). However, some also reported being sad-dened in seeing "all those tents stretched up over wooden platforms. That's something you never seen in Oklahoma—people living in tents." By constructing tents, and tents without screens at that, the government planners had neglected to take into account mosquitos and other insects that ravaged campers or the wild swings in weather that often made life for campers absolutely miserable (Cannon 12).

Before platforms were finally constructed, tents on the bare ground were destroyed in rainstorms, and for those that withstood the down-pours, campers were often left sleeping in water and mud, even within their tents. High winds often caused tents to collapse or be blown away completely. And in the summer months, the oppressive heat left mi-grants no choice but to find the only cool place in the whole camp to sleep—the floor of the community bathroom facility. Security and priva-cy were also major concerns for campers, as stray dogs often found their way into tents, as did thieves. Campers often complained of clothing, gasoline, and other necessities, as well as their few remaining luxuries, like jewelry and family heirlooms, being stolen from within their tents. One woman reported that fellow campers would gladly "take your gro-ceries" if given the chance. Finally, in an attempt to solve the tent prob-lems, the government poured cement slabs and built tin shelters at Arvin, the camp referred to as Weedpatch in the novel. While the new tin cabins did help to keep campers and their supplies dry during bouts of rain, residents discovered that rain pelting a metal roof and walls was intoler-ably noisy. And though the constructions had windows for ventilation, campers complained that summertime heat was even worse than in the tents. One camper recalled, "The wall was tin. The top was tin. You'd freeze to death in the wintertime . . . and you'd burn up in the summer-time" (Cannon 12–15). Like so many government solutions, more prob-lems are often the unintended result, which invariably require more government solutions.

While these ideas often sound effective on paper, New Deal programs like the "Farm Security Administration camps were as much a political symbol as a practical answer to the problems of farm labor" (Gregory 71n). One relief project was to be a rehabilitation camp for migrants of 100 homes, a "dream city" as dubbed by its organizers. Instead it became a "deserted village." *Baltimore Sun* journalist Frank R. Kent wrote at the time, "At least it would be deserted if there had ever been any inhabitants to desert. But there never were. There are thirty-eight lovely homesteads on the place, with material on hand for as many more. And not a soul has occupied a single one of the houses" (296). One Nebraska farmer, in 1935, could see the waste of these government projects from a mile away: "I predict that in time these homes will all be abandoned and stand as a gruesome monument to the government's inefficiency and folly and fostering a movement that to a practical mind has the earmarks of failure from the start" (Folsom 70). Steinbeck understandably chose to leave this side of the government camp story out of his novel.

After being unable to find worthwhile employment at the government camp, the Joads travel to a farm camp called Hooper ranch, where they work picking peaches. The author describes their living arrangements in their small, box-like accommodation: "The floor was splashed with grease. In the one room stood a rusty tin stove and nothing more. The tin stove rested on four bricks and its rusty stovepipe went up through the roof. The room smelled of sweat and grease." Rose of Sharon seems disgusted by the home and says, "I like the tent better," referring to the government camp they just left. But Ma reminds her that "This got a floor. . . . This here wouldn' leak when it rains" (Steinbeck, *The Grapes of Wrath* 474). While we must accept Steinbeck's harsh description as indicative of some camps at the time, we should also acknowledge that others existed that were both more comfortable and that encouraged more reliable work from laborers. In a 1939 article, journalist Frank J. Taylor writes,

> On many of the larger farms . . . the owners provide housing as good as FSA demonstration communities and for less. On the Tagus Ranch, H. C. Merritt offers two hundred permanent families neat little cottages for $3 to $5 per month, including a plot of ground for a garden. . . . Mr. Merritt's attitude toward federal camps is typical. "If my workmen live on the ranch and I tell them to be on hand at eight in the morning to pick peaches, they're on hand," he said. "If they're in a federal camp, I don't know whether they'll be here or not." (16–17)

If employment and income were what workers desired, government camps, as shown in both the novel and in historical accounts, were often a poorer solution than private camps.

But it was not as if camps were the only option available for migrants. Those workers with slightly more resources often opted for buying their own property, their sense of independence, investment, and personal responsibility figuring more heavily than their desire for government assistance. In his definitive historical account of the Okie migration to California, *American Exodus*, James N. Gregory describes how farm workers sometimes managed to purchase their own homes, despite their often terrible financial circumstances. This occurred because of the initiative of capitalists. With land valued cheaply in the suburbs of many California communities, real estate developers sectioned unused land and sold it at low prices to new buyers, often migrants. Though most lots did not have water or sewers or electricity, the excellent price and the symbol of ownership outweighed the lack of modern conveniences. For just a few dollars down, even families struggling to survive on low incomes became land owners. (70). "Property, even just a vacant lot upon which a house would someday stand," Gregory writes, "symbolized much of what had recently eluded them. It was the land they no longer or had never been able to own. . . . It was the security that they along with so many other Depression-era Americans craved" (75). Let us not forget that this home-ownership opportunity, and the accompanying sense of sanctuary and accomplishment, was produced by capitalist landowners and capital-seeking laborers.

To see this process of the capitalist process in action, Taylor, again in his 1939 article, suggests taking a look at the town of Salinas:

> The first Okies in the area squatted in squalor outside the town until an enterprising wheat farmer divided his ranch into half-acre lots, which he offered at $250 apiece, $5 down, $5 a month. The Okies snapped them up and strutted around, proud of their property ownership. . . . Some of the Okies are living in neat little three- to five-room cottages. The Okies of Little Oklahoma City are fortunate. They muscled into the lettuce-packing game and now have virtually a monopoly around Salinas, earning from 50 to 60 cents an hour for eight or nine months of the year. In that one community, three thousand migrants have achieved a respectable standard of living. (18–19)

Taylor adds that the Oklahomans' success is achievable by others as well, and should serve as not only an inspiration to other migrants, but as "an answer to the broad accusations hurled so heedlessly in *The Grapes of Wrath*" (19). In Steinbeck's concerted effort to help his readers sympathize with the Joads' desperation and root for their prosperity, his omission of actual examples of success and competing historical evidence may ultimately undermine his message.

In challenging the historical and economics presentation of the Dust Bowl era in the novel, we can also see how some of Steinbeck's descriptions truly affected migrant laborers, symbolized by the Joads, as well as those firmly settled in both Oklahoma and California. Many American citizens have felt that Steinbeck's thematic elements, characterization, tone, and other aspects of the writing come off as condescending and degrading to those who actually lived through the difficulties described in the text. Gregory writes, "Falling into the trap of pre-modernism that snared many other sympathizers, John Steinbeck in *The Grapes of Wrath* crafted a portrait that many former Dust Bowl migrants have long regarded as demeaning. . . . Poignant and powerful it is; but some former migrants wish it had never been written" (111). In his journal he kept while writing the novel, Steinbeck echoes the condescending tone felt by the actual migrants: "Got to get them out of Hooverville and into a federal camp for they must learn something of democratic procedure" (*Working Days* 64). Steinbeck's egoism in assuming that migrants must be instructed by the government on how to properly live their own lives was mirrored in the attitude of his close friend, Tom Collins, a government camp manager, who is portrayed by the helpful and sympathetic Jim Rawley in the novel. In Collins's government reports and in his notes to Steinbeck, Collins viewed the Oklahomans as "quaint and helpless" and thought that they "presented a portrait of the migrants as simple people unaccustomed to the complexities of modern life" (Gregory 108–9). In response, one Oklahoman states that "the book made Oklahomans look like a bunch of ignorant people who had never seen a pencil or a piece of paper." Gregory further explains this misrepresentation:

> It is not that there were no semi-literate, backward folk among the migrants who came to California, but rather that Steinbeck, like so many other observers, failed to convey that the majority were different. *The Grapes of Wrath*, for all its good intentions, ironically helped to solidify some of the unfortunate images which Californians already associated with the newcomers from that region. (111)

One woman believes that it is difficult to move beyond Steinbeck's often erroneous presentation of migrants: "I think the stigmatism of Steinbeck's *Grapes of Wrath* will always be with us" (111).

Much of the conflict during this era can be attributed to competing visions of two very different types of men. One, with immense amounts of formal education, thought he knew best how to plan the lives of millions of Americans; the other, likely with little more than the knowledge he had gained from the land, could tell instantly that the government programs would never be as successful as hoped. Rexford Tugwell, one of the primary players in New Deal agricultural policy, went to college, then graduate school, and had a Ph.D.—he had spent most of his time in a classroom, not in the real world of farming. His numerous government initiatives commanded a $250 million budget without actually having to produce value—as a number of his plans completely flopped at taxpayer expense—thereby undercutting private farmers and businessmen who were struggling to hang on to their livelihoods during the 1930s. Rather than facing the yearly struggle of weather, pestilence, or just weak crops, Tugwell had a comfortable job in Washington with access to the president, and he could leave it at any time for a professorship that awaited him at Columbia University, where he would earn a yearly salary that exceeded what 97 percent of other Americans earned at the time (Folsom 73). To add one final example of how a prominent persona's academic mindset could be so deleterious, President Roosevelt himself also ran a farm in his hometown of Hyde Park, New York. However, his farm "lost money every year—and he even deducted his losses on his income tax. Those deductions gave the government less revenue to operate the many federal programs the president supported" (75). Yet, Steinbeck writes that the Joads and their fellow farmers are mad at the bankers and land-owners rather than the federal government that encourages them to act in the ways they do.

Historically, it has not been crises in capitalism that have led to government interventionism. Ludwig von Mises explains that the follow-ers of interventionist doctrine believe devastating results like unemploy-ment, poverty, and famine are caused by the inherent failures of capital-ism.

> As they see it, it is precisely these disasters that clearly demonstrate the necessity of intensifying interventionism. The failures of the interven-tionist policies do not in the least impair the popularity of the implied doctrine. They are so interpreted as to strengthen, not to lessen, the prestige of these teachings. As a vicious economic theory cannot be simply refuted by historical experience, the interventionist propagan-dists have been able to go on in spite of all the havoc they have spread. (*Human Action* 851)

The dangerous policies of enacted economic interventionism are unfortu-nately promulgated by the literary analyses of anti-capitalism.

According to the Austrian strand of literary analysis, the condemna-tion of private property is diametrically opposed to the promotion of opportunity and justice for laborers and families. It is the very lack of privatization, and the over-reaching of government planners, that cause the Joads' plight. Admittedly, capitalism can be difficult for some to navi-gate, particularly when personal resources (such as flexible work skills, available cash, steady health, etc.) are lacking at certain points in time. But the freedom to choose how and where to work, the freedom to buy and sell, and the freedom to take risks and seek earned rewards far out-weigh the often disastrous repercussions of central planning by interven-tionist governments. The Joads are not victims of greedy corporate finan-ciers; rather, they are pawns in the struggle between authority and auton-omy. The government wants power to organize its citizenry; businesses want the independence to trade goods and services as they see fit for the success of their industry. The Joads, and the millions like them, are—unfortunately and incorrectly—left pointing fingers at enemies they can see instead of the ones they can't.

There is no doubt that *The Grapes of Wrath* is a masterful work of pathos. The reader falls in love with nearly every Joad character and grows to despise anyone who stands in the family's way. Steinbeck's presentation of community and of the notion that sticking together helps all to prosper is a powerful and noble message that, for many, defines the beauty of America as a nation of ambitious, hard-working, caring people who are merely trying to make it in this life and attempting to provide for the next generation. But even that perspective is challenged by a free-market economic reading of *The Grapes of Wrath*. Clearly, one of Steinbeck's goals in his novel is the promotion of community support, that by helping our neighbor in times of trouble, all citizens benefit. However, the government policies that Steinbeck extolls in the book actually diminished the role of the helpful neighbor and, instead, led to a decrease in personal and voluntary assistance to those in need. Economists Jonathan Gruber, from the Massachusetts Institute of Technology, and Daniel Hungerman, from the University of Notre Dame, report that private charitable giving during the Great Depression years decreased by 30 percent. They have discovered, after adjusting for falling incomes during the period, that this steep decline in charity was directly caused by the increase in government spending from New Deal programs. This should not be surprising, for if the government simply appropriates funds from private citizens for public spending, then there is little desire to be voluntarily generous. Therefore, the community concern and increased support from other citizens that Steinbeck desperately hoped for in his novel actually faded during the 1930s, replaced by a behemoth, faceless government bureaucracy that diminished the individual compassion of Americans. Unfortunately for Steinbeck and his anti-capitalist fans, the larger the government grows, the smaller the private citizen becomes.

Questioning the real world accuracy of the historical conflicts presented in the novel does not diminish the work as an outstanding piece of art or as a seminal text in the story of our country. A capitalist-oriented criticism simply allows the reader to more fully understand the historical and economic context of the Great Depression, as well as the motivations and emotions of the novel's characters. I hope that recognizing how greedy capitalism was not the primary culprit for the Joads' struggles offers the reader a deeper comprehension of the confusion felt by farmers of the time and a more cautious view of the involvement of national government in the lives of individual citizens and private businesses.

FIVE

Bigger's World

Urban Economics in Native Son

After examining capitalism from the viewpoints of individualism, business representations, and government influence, in the fourth literary analysis undertaken here, I will focus on social interactions, particularly in an urban environment. Human action is based upon an untold number of factors, the majority of which no one can ever know. Even the person doing the acting is scarcely aware of their complexity. Therefore, judging intentions based upon psychology (what individuals or groups may or may not be thinking regarding their activities) is a virtually impossible task that capitalism, and particular the Austrian perspective on it, purposely avoids due to the inherent complications of human agency. As Ludwig von Mises notes, "The field of our science is human action, not the psychological events which results in a human action" (*Human Action* 11–12). This task is made even more difficult when trying to understand the motivations of millions of people that inhabit a metropolitan area or migrate across vast areas to pursue their individually unique opportunities. Richard Wright's *Native Son* offers us an excellent example of how we fail in judging groups of people without knowing important information that influences causes and effects of large-scale societal behavior. A capitalistic reading allows us a clearer understanding of how activities that appear to be caused by pernicious social structures are actually the result of logical human responses to economic incentives.

This chapter will offer a perspective that may be controversial for some, as it reflects upon issues that have caused anguish for American citizens since the nation's founding. And while the intersection of race and class has become more thoroughly understood and many most affected by these social and cultural complications have made great strides forward, we remain troubled by the implications brought about by reconciling the status of the individual with her difficult surroundings. Some may argue that presenting a position in which certain individuals must be held accountable for their actions—despite unfair opportunities, discriminatory policies, and dehumanizing circumstances—is at best uninformed, and at worst blatantly racist. Such criticisms are understandable, as we all have witnessed the trials of various groups attempting to assimilate into a larger culture or reaffirm their unique identities. However, from an economic perspective that seeks to understand individual choices regarding action as separate from psychological rationale, such as the Austrian method, we must examine factual results and temper our assumptions of the causes of those results.

To demonstrate that racial perspectives do not go hand in hand with economic beliefs—further highlighting the individualist nature of Austrian economic methodology—two of the most renowned critics of the type of urban environment depicted in *Native Son* I will cite in the following pages are African Americans who, like Bigger Thomas, grew up in inner-city slums in northern metropolises. They lived through the Great Depression, faced the same racial conditions as Bigger, and after adhering with Marxist and leftist visions of urban economic life as young men, later developed a clearer understanding of the complicated nature of human action. Thomas Sowell and Walter Williams are economists who have served at prestigious universities, on government research committees, and in the private sector. They have each authored numerous books on poverty, discrimination, public policy, and have researched nearly every facet of urban and racial economics, from housing to wages, crime to education. Their expertise is invaluable, and while their own cultural background is not the topic of discussion here, their research is highly illuminating for this chapter. While not ignoring the difficulties of racial dynamics, like Sowell, Williams, and other economists cited here, I aim to bring to light the responsibility of the individual and a clarified vision of historical circumstances, thus hoping to gain a larger comprehension of the characters and setting of this novel.

Bigger Thomas, the troubled protagonist of Wright's novel, inhabits a world where racism lurks on every street and inopportunity hovers like a cloud over his existence. Bigger's neighborhood on the South Side of Chicago resembles a prison, similar to the one he inhabits at the novel's conclusion, except that instead of bars, he is restrained by fear, and instead of cold concrete, he is surrounded by confusion of the world around him. He interprets the world through oppressed eyes, and we are asked by Bigger, the lawyer Boris Max, and by Wright himself to observe how blacks seem to be inescapably condemned to neighborhood barriers, menial occupations, and an inequality of life. Through Bigger's tragic circumstances, Wright asks us to see Bigger for what whites have made him—a monster of a boy with no independence of mind or spirit of purpose. His environment, ruled by whites and capitalistic ideology, has angered and bewildered him to the point of ultimate rebellion. It is this environment that has influenced generations of blacks to conform to the place in society that whites have seemingly destined for them. It is this environment that offers no peace and fosters no hope.

The Chicago of 1940 that Wright describes and Bigger Thomas inhabits is one in which lynch mobs prowl for black criminals, newspapers are strongly bigoted, businesses are discriminatory, whites use their economic and racial superiority to take advantage of blacks, and blacks have no opportunities for upward mobility. "Like *Grapes of Wrath*," one contemporary critic writes of *Native Son*, "it is a fully realized story of unfortunates, uncompromisingly realistic, and quite as human as it is Negro" (qtd. in Gloster 234). While this may have been true for some people at some times in some places, the overall facts of history and economic action largely belie Wright's setting. When examining Bigger's surroundings, we must also consider the historical context of 1930s Chicago as well as Wright's portrayal of plausible day-to-day individual interactions that lead to wider economic patterns. Many readers will decry the power dynamics, oppressive practices, and various inequalities portrayed in the novel, but these discrepancies do ultimately stem from logically motivated economic factors. We should not neglect important elements of literary and historical analysis that can lead to alternative and likewise informed interpretations of the text at hand. Such will be the study that follows here.

One example of how documented facts of historical context may contradict Bigger's perception of victimization occurs early in the text, as Bigger complains that he would like to go to pilot school but is not allowed due to his race. In reality, while it was extremely difficult for blacks to enter the field of aviation in the interwar period, Bigger's presumption that no blacks were allowed to fly is not completely accurate. Pioneering black pilot C. Alfred Anderson, who in 1941 took First Lady Eleanor Roosevelt on a flight to substantiate the Tuskegee Experiment, earned his pilot license in 1929. Even black women could obtain pilot licenses, as Willa Brown demonstrated in 1938. And there were many more examples of such trailblazers. Sociologist Philip Hart has written extensively on the history of black aviation in the 1920s and 1930s. His book *Flying Free: America's First Black Aviators* (1992) and his PBS film *Flyers in Search of a Dream* (1987) thoroughly explore the fascinating legacy of black pilots. And of course, in the years immediately following *Native Son*'s publication, the black pilots of the Tuskegee Airmen made history as heroes in World War II, though they battled extreme racial prejudice and had to wait until near the end of the war to demonstrate their mettle. With closer examination of the social, political, and cultural contexts, I offer additional economic insights about the novel. To explore the economics of Bigger's setting is to more thoroughly understand

Bigger's difficulties in comprehending (and Wright's presentation of) the novel's fuller sociohistorical context.

Native Son certainly holds an important place in American literature, as well for the literary criticism that accompanies it. Postcolonial criticism, critical race studies, and other modes of analysis have benefited greatly from Wright's novel. Frantz Fanon's famous essay "The Fact of Blackness" (1952) mentions Bigger Thomas as he highlights the understandable complications of blacks inhabiting predominantly white environments, and the accompanying psychological and social negotiations that have defined the black experience for large parts of Western history. Literary critic Irving Howe, in his 1963 article "Black Boys and Native Sons," situated Wright among other prominent black voices, like James Baldwin, and examined Wright's authorial significance as one who both revealed and developed black culture in the literary form. While those forms of criticism are indispensable for the broader examination of *Native Son*, this chapter, in keeping with the overall theme of this project, will focus more narrowly on the economic presentation of capitalism and its accompanying systemic implications. Traditional economic readings of *Native Son* emphasize Bigger's socially constructed sense of self-worth, as dictated to him by not only an unfair racial environment, but by the oppressively overarching capitalistic superstructure. Such readings are, quite fairly, founded in the ideology of the author himself. It is easy to see the pervasive anti-capitalist ideology presented in *Native Son*, and Wright validated his own perspective by stating, "from 1932 to 1944 I was a member of the Communist Party of the United States" (qtd. in Brignano 53). Influenced by the reading of Marxist materials, Wright drew a connection between the social experiences of blacks and lower-class laborers, a connection that defines the narrative ethos of *Native Son* (55). Wright believed that his writing could and should form a revolutionary economic argument:

> A Marxist analysis of society . . . creates a picture which, when placed before the eyes of the writer, should unify his personality, organize his emotions, buttress him with a tense and obdurate will to change the world. And, in turn, this changed world will dialectically change the writer. Hence, it is through a Marxist conception of reality and society that the maximum degree of freedom in thought and feeling can be gained for the Negro writer. (qtd. in Shulman 138)

Brignano also notes of Wright's early writings that "Not only are they tinged with a bitter hatred for all capitalistic institutions and representatives, but they contain a multitude of violent images and actions" (56). Wright's feelings for Marxism fluctuated later in his life, but his Marxist economic philosophy pertains directly to *Native Son*.

Those Marxist beliefs are represented in Bigger's feelings of displacement and powerlessness, as well as the representation of the economic disparities in Bigger's world. Bigger's greatest challenge is his under-standing of self and his relationship to those social groups and institu-tions around him. And it is capitalism's inherent power dynamics through which some (blacks, in this novel) are oppressed and others (whites, in this novel) are protected. Wright has clearly indicated that "[f]raming the superstructure of society dominated by the white world is capitalism, which is a force that smothers and denudes the individual personality" (Brignano 23). The individualism that is so vital to economic growth is subsumed, according to anti-capitalist critics, by the hegemony of capitalistic ideology. Robert Shulman writes that "Bigger lives in a competitive, capitalistic society where self-worth depends significantly on how much a person owns, with the freedom of movement and choice that go along with money" (139). Bigger's perception of feeling trapped, both economically and emotionally, is indicative of this absence of per-sonal freedom. "In a society of possessive individualism," Shulman con-tinues, "the ownership and control of property are the preconditions for the ownership of psychic capital, the psychological and personal freedom basic to a sense of self-worth in America" (153). It is this perceived lack of self-ownership and identity with which Bigger struggles throughout the novel. Because he has no control over property, including himself, he cannot function according to the norms of the white, capitalistic structure that envelops him and, by extension, blacks in 1940 Chicago and through-out much of American history.

We witness even more clearly the condemnation of capitalism in the language of Max, Bigger's lawyer, and particularly in Max's final speech in the courtroom. Max makes it clear that Bigger's life has not only been defined by his race, but perhaps more importantly by his class, through the exploitation of capitalists. Max tells Bigger,

> They hire people and they don't pay them enough; they take what people own and build up power. They rule and regulate life. They have things arranged so that they can do those things and the people can't fight back. They do that to black people more than others because they say that black people are inferior. But, Bigger, they say that *all* people who work are inferior. (Wright 500)

Wright uses the courtroom scene to have Max attempt to "expose capital-ism as the root of Bigger's unpremeditated crime. . . . Through Max, Wright undoubtedly is attacking capitalism and offering in its place the vision of a brighter, happier society" (Brignano 81).

When determining whether racism or discrimination or lack of oppor-tunity occurs, however, we must examine various economic factors, put-ting aside temporarily our expectation that it can all be written off to an asymmetrical white/black power dynamic. Historically, there was declin-ing antagonism between northern blacks and whites during the nine-teenth century, and this did not reverse itself in newfound hostility dur-

ing the twentieth century. Any such reactionary twentieth-century perspective cannot be simply attributed to white racism, particularly when
the black migration from the South was denounced so heavily by *black*
northerners and newspapers. Rather, there were real-world economic
factors that led multiple social groups, among and across races, to change
their proactive and reactive behaviors, leading to patently unfair but perfectly predictable repercussions.

During this time, ironically, as white barriers against blacks increased,
so did black barriers against other blacks. Proper social behavior, much
emphasized by black elites, carried as much cultural currency as money
or light skin color. Blacks who had lived in the North for a generation or
more and become acclimated to social norms saw equality among races
increase greatly. The censuring by blacks of blacks' improper behavior
was not isolated to major cities in the North. The West also deprecated
the poor manners of black southerners. San Francisco and Portland, two
cities long free of Jim Crow laws, eventually succumbed to some discriminatory legislation, in part because native blacks, who had long been law-
abiding and self-sustaining, were offended by the newcomers' loud and
angry behavior and resented their uneducated and ill-mannered presence (Sowell, *Black* 49). Blacks understandably did not want to see their
increased social standing tarnished. In many northern cities, where black
voting had once been illegal, blacks were voting by the 1880s and even
elected to public office by the 1890s. High schools and colleges were
largely integrated, and despite their small representative population,
public restrictions were expunged from the law. Therefore, at the end of
the nineteenth century in the North, white opinion of and cooperation
with blacks were generally increasing, to the point that "communities
were themselves becoming cleaner, safer, and more orderly during this
era of improving race relations" (Sowell, *Black* 46).

When Richard Wright himself arrived in Chicago in 1927, he said, "I
looked about to see if there were signs saying: FOR WHITE—FOR COL-
ORED. I saw none. Black people and white people moved about, each
seemingly intent upon his private mission. There was no racial fear"
(Thernstrom and Thernstrom 55). Strangely, it is nevertheless fear that
Wright uses as the main impetus for the doom that finds his most famous
literary character, Bigger Thomas, and it is the familiar animus against
white oppression that Wright locates in Bigger. Wright discovered that
while discrimination did exist, as it does in some forms in all places,
"What he did not find in Chicago was a system of racial and social control designed to inspire terror." One black migrant to Chicago comment-
ed that he "had a chance to be a man regardless of [your] color" (Thernstrom and Thernstrom 55). Whites in Chicago did not call blacks "boy" or
"uncle," and blacks there did not call whites both young and old "mister"
(56). Blacks did not have to enter white homes through the back door;
they dined together; they shook hands; and they were not forced to the

back of lines. Wright himself noted how he was able to buy a paper at a crowded newsstand before all the whites. Blacks could and did hold public office in Chicago, black citizens were encouraged to vote by politicians eager to earn their vote, and it was not unusual for whites to vote for black candidates. Blacks held many important positions on Chicago city councils, as judges, as city prosecutors, as state's attorneys, and as members of the Illinois state legislature (Thernstrom and Thernstrom 55). Oscar de Priest, a Republican, served from 1929 to 1935 as the first black in the U.S. House of Representatives in the modern era, and he was from Bigger Thomas's own neighborhood on the South Side. Blacks were clearly a legitimate social and political constituency in 1940 Chicago.

The "Great Migration" of southern blacks like Bigger Thomas into northern cities in the early decades of the twentieth century, however, overwhelmed the native northern black and white populations. The black population in Chicago alone grew by over 800 percent between 1900 and 1940. Similarly rapid population growth occurred in other northern cities, as well. Their numbers were difficult to accommodate, but it was their strange "behavior patterns that shocked both blacks and whites." Black northerners and black newspapers alike criticized the migrants as "vulgar, rowdy, unwashed, and criminal." Violent crime and illegitimate births among the new migrant blacks increased rapidly across northern cities (Sowell, *Black* 47). Consequently, there was significant retrogression in northern race relations, driven by a backlash against what was perceived as socially threatening behavior among immigrant blacks, as well as the perceived shrinking of job opportunities, a rapidly growing labor pool, and the threat to the racialized boundaries of Chicago.

The oppressive racial environment that Bigger experiences in 1930s Chicago was not a result of decades of social inequality, but was a relatively recent social development. Up until 1920, what was known as "Black Belt" of Chicago was not overwhelmingly black. Though 90 percent of blacks in the entire city lived there, blacks were roughly only 55 percent of total population in that section of town. And for decades, whites and blacks lived largely harmoniously and without major incident, with the major exception of the 1919 "Red Summer" riots that embroiled Chicago and other northern cities. Nevertheless, the Chicago Commission on Race Relations that was set up in the wake of those postwar riots reported that neighbors of different races looked after each other, shared doctors and schools and stores, and even worked together on community projects (108–13). One white resident who had lived in the Black Belt for forty years said, "I have never had more honest, quiet, and law-abiding neighbors than those who are of the African race. . . . There is no race question; it is a question of intelligence and morality, pure and simple" (109). And a number of black residents were reported to have reciprocated those types of comments. One black woman stated that the courtesy of whites toward her was "all that could be desired," and another stated that the surrounding white families "treat my family right" (110).

While there certainly was racial friction in the city, particularly between Irish whites and blacks, the growth and development of the black community of Chicago proceeded along expected lines throughout the early twentieth century. E. Franklin Frazier, a highly influential black sociologist of the era and an expert in Chicago's racial climate, noted that blacks organized themselves in ways similar to other racial and cultural groups: distinction within the black population "was part of the general process of segregation of different racial, economic, and cultural groups . . . on the basis of occupation, intelligence, and ambition" (257). An editor for a black newspaper in Chicago wrote that internal segregation among blacks was "proceeding along its natural course exactly analogous, or at least similar, to the formation of social groups of the white race of this country" (qtd. in Gatewood 124).

As blacks arrived in Chicago during the Great Migration, they settled in neighborhoods that in turn delineated their residents' cultural segregation among the black population as a whole. The center of the city became home for the newest migrants from the South, just like Bigger. Over 77 percent of the heads of these families were former southerners, and the percentage of these families decreased concentrically outwards as the black community grew (Frazier 258). The same pattern held true regarding literacy and ancestry. The center of the city had the highest level of illiteracy and of unmixed African-American heritage. Radiating outward in the city were those with higher literacy and more mixed race heritage. According to Frazier, these residential patterns "coincided with an increase in the proportion of Negroes in professional and clerical occupations and in business" (260). Mulatto neighborhoods had lower crime rates, and their members were on average more highly educated, had better jobs, had better housing, and had more wealth than those in other black communities. This social environment tended to encourage both racial mixing and the formation of a socially exclusive class (Sowell, *Black* 44).

Some blacks had become quite economically successful, even forming a kind of black aristocracy in Chicago, as well as other cities in the North. These upper-class blacks did not receive new blacks or whites from the South well. The enormous black influx from the South furthered "class stratification among Chicago's blacks," whereby many in the black upper class "resisted the mass migration into their city" (Gatewood 122). For established blacks, "Their education and good breeding prompted them to look with displeasure on the less-decorous behavior and lifestyles of blacks in social strata below them" (119). One wealthy black woman said she refused to "mingle with ill-bred people," whatever their race. Another wealthy black aristocrat reported that the upper-class black population in Chicago was "better dressed, better housed, and better mannered

shoplifting or vandalism are greater than usual, or costs such as insurance or security are greater than usual, prices are also likely to be higher in order to compensate for the extenuating expenses of the location. In a rough neighborhood, where broken windows, security cameras, and higher rates of shipping must be covered, higher prices of goods are the result (Sowell, *The Economics* 163). Walter Williams concurs:

> To view the merchants' behavior as exploitative or racist ignores the fact that ghettos tend to present a high-cost business environment. . . . Much of the behavior that critics have condemned is merely an economic response to an environment that raises the cost of doing business. If products and services are to be provided in the ghetto, prices must reflect their higher costs. (31)

Logically, if such businesses were gouging their black customers, this would normally lead to the opening of new businesses that would be interested in obtaining high profits. However, the opposite occurs in most urban areas, as businesses usually leave without being replaced. Furthermore, black-owned businesses in the ghetto nearly always charge at least as much for services as white-owned businesses. This further discounts the belief in racism among inner-city businesses (31–32). Those who are not criminals most often pay the price for those who are. Bigger Thomas is a criminal himself, which causes stores to raise prices as a way to protect against the higher costs associated with criminals like Bigger. Bigger has the audacity to complain about prices, which are likely raised because of the precise criminal behavior he inflicts on the community. It's not purely racism; it's also economics.

Criminal actions like those that Bigger and his friends perform early in the novel, as well as Bigger's ultimate double homicide, inflict drastic long-term consequences upon a community, particularly among blacks themselves, as economic evidence has shown. In one major northern city at the end of the nineteenth century, the black-on-black murder rate was five and a half times the white-on-white murder rate (Thernstrom and Thernstrom 261). Even by the end of the twentieth century, when race relations were much improved compared to the first decades of the 1900s, "more blacks than whites—59 percent versus 52 percent—agreed that blacks were 'aggressive or violent.'" According to one survey, "52 percent of African Americans and 31 percent of whites were afraid to walk alone at night in their neighborhoods," and "72 percent of blacks (but only 64 percent of whites) reported thinking that Chicago was dangerous" (260). In 2011, the U.S. Department of Justice reported that from 1980 to 2008, 93 percent of blacks who were murdered were killed by fellow blacks (Cooper and Smith 13). Though white-on-white murder rates are nearly as high (84 percent, demonstrating that race and crime are often simply linked by proximity), the black victimization rate is six times more than the white victimization rate (11). This shows that not only are blacks hardly ever being attacked by "racist" whites, blacks are harming one another at much higher rates than when whites harm one another.

Furthermore, there is evidence that suggests this criminality is not caused exclusively or primarily by environmental conditions. Homicides increased dramatically between 1900 and 1929. However, during the Great Depression, when unemployment spiked and citizens were at their poorest and most frustrated, homicides *dropped* by 25 percent and continued to do so through the 1940s and 1950s. Then, when civil rights legislation came into full effect in the 1960s, when race relations, equality, and shared prosperity should have helped all Americans improve their lives, the rate for all violent crimes—rape, robbery, assault, and homicide— skyrocketed. Violent crime doubled during the 1960s and rose another 60 percent in the 1970s (Thernstrom and Thernstrom 261–62). Clearly, not all difficult economic and social conditions breed violence. During some of the most trying times, violence decreased, and during some of the times of improved equality—as virtually no one would argue that life for minorities was *better* during Bigger's era—violence among blacks, sadly, either persisted or increased.

Bigger and his lawyer explain that he had no choice but to commit crime, and that his environment is a fertile breeding ground for such behavior. Hugh Gloster notes that "The all-pervading thought of *Native Son* is that a prejudiced and capitalistic social order, rather than any intrinsic human deficiency, is the cause of the frustration and rebellion of underprivileged Negro youth of America" (232). However, economist and historian Thomas Sowell adamantly disagrees: "Poverty, unemployment, and racial discrimination are frequently listed among the prime 'root causes' of riots and other criminality among blacks." A study of economic causes and effects proves the opposite to be true, according to Sowell: it is not these community conditions that cause crime; rather, crime causes neighborhoods to become riddled with these conditions (*Economic Facts* 166–67). One example among many of these economic patterns took place in another primarily black community just a few decades after *Native Son*, as urban race riots during the 1960s could be read to illustrate how conditions are a *result*, not a cause, of poor behavior. In Detroit in the 1960s,

> The poverty rate among Detroit's black population was only half of that of blacks nationwide, its homeownership rate among blacks was the highest in the country, and its unemployment rate was 3.4 percent—lower than that among *whites* nationwide. Detroit did not have a massive riot because it was an economic disaster area. It became an economic disaster area *after* the riots, as did black neighborhoods in many other cities across the country. Moreover, riot-torn neighborhoods in these cities remained disaster areas for decades thereafter, as businesses became reluctant to locate there, reducing access to both

jobs and places to shop, and both black and white middle-class people left for the suburbs. (167)

As Sowell summarizes, "Inner city ghettos had lower rates of crime and violence, as well as lower unemployment rates, and most black children grew up in two-parent households" *before* the supposed racial improvements of the 1960s (22). Arguably, the worst urban conditions are actually in the very cities where residents ignore the real world economic consequences of their actions, usually leading to more social breakdowns and violence.

One of the worst kinds of violence that has befallen our nation is the act of lynching. However, as tragic and horrific as lynchings have been to American history, we must not presume that Wright's depiction of Bigger's flight from violent mobs was typical for the time period or location. According to the archives at the Tuskegee Institute, there were only a *total* of thirty-four lynchings in Illinois between 1882 and 1968. And likely to the surprise of many, the victims were split between the races— nineteen black, fifteen white. It should go without saying that any number above zero is too many lynchings, but in 1940, the year of Bigger's demise, there were only four black lynchings in the entire country ("Lynching"). In fact, before the Civil War, the majority of lynchings in America were against *whites* (Gibson).

Richard Wright sees a very different and much more threatening picture. He characterizes the lynching mentality in his presentation of the *Chicago Tribune* and its reporting of actual cases where the paper showed derogatory and dehumanizing depictions of blacks. While the *Chicago Tribune* did occasionally show disturbing racial bias in its reporting, the paper was also a leading publication in condemning lynching, as indicated by the press clipping about Bigger Thomas (Perloff 323). Decades earlier, during the Civil War, the paper was strongly abolitionist. And though the publication did sometimes print cruel remarks towards blacks, as the novel presents, the *Chicago Tribune* also ran strong anti-Catholic and anti-Irish editorials years earlier (Funchion). Therefore, blacks were not necessarily singled out, as Wright seems to portray.

As newspapers covered lynchings, some important political leaders of the 1930s seemed, unfortunately, to be unmoved. One of these was the liberal icon Franklin D. Roosevelt, whose Federal Writers' Project (part of Roosevelt's New Deal program) gave employment to Richard Wright. While the number of lynchings had dropped during Herbert Hoover's presidency (1929–1933), lynchings increased 40 percent during Roosevelt's first term (Folsom 207). Black Americans pleaded with Congress to take a stronger stance against this horrendous crime. However, Roosevelt refused to stand behind anti-lynching bills, and his fellow Democrats filibustered such legislation several times in the late 1930s (206). To avoid offending southern Democrats, he even refused to schedule a meeting with Walter White, chief spokesman for the NAACP. Shockingly, "after two black men were tortured to death by blowtorch in Mississippi, [and] a new anti-lynching bill finally did get through the House with an almost two-to-one margin, Roosevelt . . . still failed to support it" (Thernstrom and Thernstrom 67). Gallup polls at the time showed that 72 percent of northerners and 57 percent of southerners wanted the new laws making lynching a federal crime. Roosevelt's wife, Eleanor, was a powerfully vocal supporter of the bills; yet her husband continued to sit on his hands. Even as he recognized that signing anti-lynching legislation would virtually guarantee his reelection in 1936, Roosevelt chose not to take any strong position on using federal authority to defend blacks against lynching (Folsom 207).

But lynching laws were not the only areas in which Roosevelt denied support for the black community. He also refused to abolish the poll tax, which had kept blacks from voting for decades, when a constitutional amendment was offered. He also refused to stand up to the racist policies of the American Federation of Labor, which had been denying blacks from entering skilled trades (Folsom 209). Roosevelt ignored petitions to integrate his press conferences as he continued to allow the White House Correspondents' Association to admit only whites (211). He refused to invite American Olympic hero Jesse Owens to the White House after Owens proudly represented the nation in Nazi Germany in 1936, and he was largely dismissive of a number of prominent black figures (210). When he did meet with them, he "dominated the conversations and rarely gave them a chance to speak." Strangely, "Roosevelt was wary of forming close political ties to black Americans, and he used no political capital to support civil rights during the New Deal years" (211).

Roosevelt's New Deal policies harmed blacks most of all. His Agricultural Adjustment Administration greatly decreased black employment by removing land from cultivation and providing subsidies for labor-reducing farm equipment. Southern Democrats made sure that agricultural workers and domestic servants, who were mostly blacks, were denied financial protection through the Social Security Act of 1935 (Thernstrom and Thernstrom 63). The National Industrial Recovery Act of 1933 and the Fair Labor Standards Act of 1938 also harmed blacks disproportionately. These labor laws imposed minimum wage standards that most adversely affected those with lesser education and skills, which were often minorities. While black employment in government jobs did increase dramatically under Roosevelt, black employment in the private sector languished. Upwards of 500,000 blacks became unemployed due to the policies of the National Recovery Administration—"making it, in the view of the black press, a 'Negro Removal Act'" (64).

Many of these disastrous social policies that harm blacks are still in effect today and continue to be tremendously detrimental to the very segments of the American population they intend to help. Perhaps the most telling fact of blacks' role in their own demise through their ill-fated trust in government is that "Of all the groups that switched to the Democratic party in the 1930s, none moved as dramatically as blacks, 76 percent of whom cast their ballots for FDR in 1936" (Thernstrom and Thernstrom 65). They were drawn to the Democratic party by the promise of jobs and the hopes of improved race relations. Troublingly, blacks flocked to the polls for the Roosevelt administration, not realizing how misplaced their trust in the New Deal might be: "During the 1930s, ironically, blacks left the party of Lincoln for the party of white supremacy" (67). Blacks in 1940 like Bigger Thomas may have voted themselves as much discrimination and harmful policies as any white Republicans could have ever bestowed upon them.

In conclusion, we must remember that the Great Migration to the North was a white migration as well as a black one. Therefore, the racist attitudes that had defined the culture of the South were brought to the North and permeated amongst social communities. Simultaneously, we can cite the complicity of blacks (and in our context here, Bigger Thomas) in their own struggles. Difficulty in acclimating to acceptable social norms, an adjustment other ethnicities had to make as well, kept blacks like Bigger Thomas mired in poverty, crime, and familial disarray. The appeal of politicians' promises kept some blacks like Bigger Thomas beholden to government rather than seeking individual achievement and personal responsibility. There are logical, economic reasons for how the world functions, and those who have not subscribed to Bigger's victim mentality have been more likely to prosper on par with other ethnicities.

An anti-capitalist reading of *Native Son* largely ignores this perspective, as indicated by the sympathetic critics who reviewed the text at the time of its publication. Upon the release of *Native Son*, the *Washington Star* said that Bigger is most definitely a victim: "He has no opportunity, says Mr. Wright, and every influence of society has acted to make his crime inevitable. Similar sentiments are put into the mouth of the lawyer at the trial" (Reilly 56). "There can be no doubt," the *Star* continued, "that Mr. Wright considers this boy typical of the vast Negro population" (57). The majority of other publications echoed these sentiments. The *Herald Tribune* stated that *Native Son* was a "deeply compassionate and understanding novel" (42). The *Saturday Review of Literature* explained that "Wright skillfully delivers our sympathies to Bigger. We feel the constricting white world around him. We share his sullen timidity . . . we resent with him . . . we stand in terror with him . . . and we run with him" (51). *New Masses* praised the work as a "brilliant analysis of the interplay of social and psychological factors in experience" (60). *Sunday Worker* wrote that Wright had a clear objective in his novel: "He wants to show the most degrading oppression of the Negro—what capitalism can do to a human being" (69). The black publication *Chicago Defender* reported of the "hope that *Native Son* shall not only focus attention upon the evils which are visited upon us, but that it shall, by the very urgency of its message, transform a rotten social, economic system into a living democracy for all" (65).

The Atlantic Monthly, however, bravely broke from the pattern of adulation and disputed the novel's immense praise: "Mr. Wright might have made a more manly and certainly more convincing case for his people if he had stuck to fact." In all states in the North, blacks had full political and voting rights. Nowhere in the North were blacks "denied equal protection of the laws" (Reilly 91). If racial or cultural oppression of members of a minority compels them to destroy those in the majority, Jews in Russia, Poland, Germany, Egypt, England, and the United States—a minority who had been oppressed far longer than black Americans—would have become the most prolific mass murderers in world history (92–93). But they did not because they chose a behavior that was above their difficult circumstances.

In line with the contemporary analysis by *The Atlantic Monthly*, an economic approach to Native Son reveals the powerful but unrecognized cause-and-effect relationships that abide for Bigger Thomas and his Chicago community. Ludwig von Mises writes,

> The individual is born at a definite date in history into a definite situation determined by geography, history, social institutions, mores, and ideologies. He has daily to face the alteration in the structure of this traditional surrounding affected by the actions of his contemporaries. He does not simply live in the world. He lives in a circumscribed spot. He is both furthered and hampered in his acting by all that is peculiar to this spot. But he is not determined by it. . . . The environment determines the situation but not the response. To the same situation different modes of reacting are thinkable and feasible. Which one the actors choose depends on their individuality. (*Theory and History* 326)

What do we think of Bigger if we acknowledge that it is not just environmental conditions that cause crime, but crime that ruins environmental conditions? What is our opinion of Bigger when we can see that blacks used their political influence to choose leadership that imposed policies that actually worsened many of their social conditions? How do we view Bigger when we can see that charges of racism in housing, business, employment, and other elements of community are often inaccurate matters of perception and should rather be viewed as logical consequences of human interaction? How much should we sympathize with Bigger if we can see that difficulties were not unique to blacks alone, but also existed for whites with a similar cultural background; and that success was not unique to whites alone, but also existed for many blacks? These queries offer an interpretation of Bigger Thomas that reduces social sympathy and emphasizes personal responsibility. Bigger is not purely a victim of circumstance, but rather a proactive, self-harming agent of misplaced anger and unfounded fear. Though he is a confused young man, he is ultimately a criminal, and one who believes blame always lies within someone else. And if readers resort solely to familiar analyses of race and class, they are in danger of becoming critics that bear a striking resemblance to Bigger Thomas—one whose social vision ignores economic reality.

While an anti-capitalist interpretation does offer an interesting and worthwhile methodology for examining certain economic, historical, and sociological relationships and institutions, I contend that such a reading obscures much of the true value of the story. Wright's emphasis on capitalistically and racially oppressive accounts of Bigger's life creates an attractive but distracting shift away from Bigger's much more intriguing psychological struggles. Bigger's complications are born out of his relationships with others—rich and poor, black and white—and to the environment they all inhabit. His confusion regarding how to deal with family, friends, his boss, and girls he finds attractive makes Bigger a character worth reading because these struggles are what make him, and all of us, distinctly human. Bigger is searching for hope, love, and personal understanding in the novel, not an abstract ideology. An anti-capitalist reading subverts the real humanity of the novel, whereas a capitalistic reading embraces the difficulties of life and how foundational these difficulties are in the human pursuit of effective action.

SIX

Rage Against the Machine

Kurt Vonnegut's Player Piano

Following World War II, the American economy flourished. From the late 1940s to the early 1970s, the United States saw Gross Domestic Product rise, unemployment rates fall, and an expansion of prosperity for all economic classes, and in particular, the middle class. The credit for such economic improvement was attributed to a variety of factions, and each had a reasonable claim to that honor. Some attributed post-war success to Keynesians, whose policies of government guidance since the onset of the Great Depression had finally seen their interventionist approach come to fruition. Higher taxes on personal incomes and business profits during the early part of the era; the prominence of the G.I. Bill; the proliferation of labor unions; and the maturation of war bonds seemed to prove that government spending helped not only to stabilize a national economy shaken by war and still reeling from depression, but to grow it exponentially. On the other hand, free-market supporters believed the oppositionist congressional policies of deregulation, removal of price controls, and sharp decreases in tax rates in the 1960s led to the post-war boom. Others, who could be associated with either economic model, believed that it was the ever-increasing strength of the American military that alleviated concerns abroad and allowed security at home to produce economic accessibility and productivity. While each interpretation of these economic conditions and consequences had some measure of validity, it was the vast proliferation of technological methods of production that posed a new threat to existing economic ideologies.

The momentum of technological advances that carried the West through the Second World War soon carried on during times of peace, creating an America in which wartime demands for more bullets and

bombers evolved into calls for more cars, televisions, and household ap-
pliances. But with the explosion of material wealth and suburban comfort
came concerns regarding what role mechanization in production was
actually playing in the lives of laborers and in the broader American
social fabric. Some began to see an automated culture displacing our
workers, segregating our citizens, and endangering our humanity. It is
this question of the effects of machinery on labor, as depicted in the work
of a prominent author and in the historical data of the mid-twentieth
century, which will be discussed in the pages that follow.

I began this book in chapters 1 and 2 by exploring the importance of
the individual, both in literary creation and in economic action. The individual's inherent power to choose for herself is the very foundation of art
and capitalistic agency. But what if the role of the individual in culture
appeared to be reduced, to be deemed, in fact, replaceable? Can humanity withstand, in a sense, a de-evolution of the individual as market participant? Kurt Vonnegut explores these questions and much more in his
first novel, *Player Piano* (1952), where he presents a dystopian America in
which machines have almost completely taken over the function of productivity. This automation creates class stratification between elites, such
as the engineers who maintain the machines, and lower class laborers,
whose jobs have largely been eliminated by the machines. The disenfran-
chised workers are left with a stagnant existence and are prompted to
foment a rebellion against the machines that govern their daily lives and
that thereby present an ominous threat to humanity's ability to achieve
self-actualization.

Vonnegut got the idea for *Player Piano* while working at General Electric Company (GE)—one of the largest and most influential corporations
in the world—as a young man. He remembers how, in 1949, computer-
ization was starting to emerge and workers were "foreseeing all sorts of
machines being run by little boxes and punched cards. *Player Piano* was
my response to the implications of having everything run by little boxes"
(Standish 93). This vocational experience became the impetus for his lean-
ings toward science fiction writing. For Vonnegut, working at "General
Electric Company *was* science fiction." But Vonnegut's work has never
been so easily categorized. Thomas P. Hoffman describes how Vonnegut's book is "more than a science fiction novel, an anti-utopian novel, or
a black humor novel"; rather, it "might also be classified as a work of
sociology expressed in fictional form because in this book Vonnegut
writes more like a social scientist than a novelist" (125). *Player Piano* being
Vonnegut's first novel, it is easy to see that the text resembles other
Vonnegut works, such as short fiction like "Unpaid Consultant," "EPI-
CAC," "Deer in the Works," and "Report on the Barnhouse Effect," and
anticipates future works such as *God Bless You, Mr. Rosewater* and *The
Sirens of Titan*. Challenging social conventions and questioning human-

ity's ability to cope with progress became hallmarks of Vonnegut's writing, helping to brand him a literary icon in the postmodern movement.

While *Player Piano* exemplifies the ironic tone and historical commentary that we often appreciate in Vonnegut, this text is not entirely successful in its effectiveness in reaching its satirical goal. Vonnegut's novel is a dystopia of not only a future America, but of an America already closely at hand. William Rodney Allen describes the novel as "an extension of 1952 rather than a radical break from it. . . . Its aim is more to satirize corporate life in the 1950s and to fantasize about a profoundly different world in the distant future" (20). However, it is difficult to determine which form of dystopia Vonnegut is actually presenting: a society in which machines have displaced human labor, or one in which government bureaucrats attempt to centralize planning of all of society's methods of production? Clearly, the former is a dystopia for anti-capitalists and other proponents of collectivism, while the latter is the dystopia of free-marketers and anti-mercantilists. Though I have already discussed the dangers of government interventionism in this book, particularly in chapters 3 and 4, let us revisit such economic activities briefly once again in order to offer an alternative reading of Vonnegut's text.

Amid varying plotlines of betrayal and revolution against the industrialized society, one of the main characters, a former government worker who becomes involved in a plot to retake control of manufacturing, comments on the complications of organizing humans according to economic models: "If only it weren't for the people, the goddamned people," says Finnerty, "always getting tangled up in the machinery. If it weren't for them, earth would be an engineer's paradise" (Vonnegut, *Player Piano* 313). Fitting with his own economic position as an avowed socialist, Vonnegut fills the novel with such overt anti-capitalist musings and criticisms of technology's influence on a booming post-war America. Marx himself once condescendingly wrote that "machinery has greatly increased the number of well-to-do idlers" (*Capital* 405n1). But it is this quote from Finnerty that encapsulates all that is wrong with the anti-capitalist ideology and demonstrates the foundational premise of the Austrian perspective. One cannot centrally plan humanity because, as Mises writes, "the main fact is that there are no constant relations" (*Human Action* 56). Economics is not like applying the physical sciences, whereby physics, mathematics, and engineering can predict phenomena and solve scientific problems. Human action does not abide by the rules of the physical world. "Experience of economic history is always experience of complex phenomena," Mises adds. "It can never convey knowledge of the kind the experimenter abstracts from a laboratory experiment" (348). Finnerty's dilemma is a valid one: it is the people who always get in the way of grand schemes. Finnerty's goals of labor revolution could thus be reinterpreted as a call to capitalism and entrepreneurship. He says, "I want to stay as close to the edge as I can without going over. Out on the edge you see all kinds of things you can't see from the center. Big, undreamed of things—the people on the edge see them first" (Vonnegut, *Player Piano* 86). It is this longing to break from overbearing bureaucracy that epitomizes a capitalistic perspective.

Vonnegut thus advocates an intriguing economic model in his novel, a form of "private socialism where the corporations, not needing to compete because of being monopolies, nevertheless are government regulated. Although there are no taxes on things, there is a heavy tax on machine labor" (Morse 30n4). Doctor Halyard, the visiting Shah's tour guide and a representative of the U.S. State Department, adamantly explains that industry is run "by a committee of leaders from private industry, not politicians" (Vonnegut, *Player Piano* 28). But we know this is only true in appearance, as the father of Paul Proteus, the novel's protagonist, once held the second most powerful position in American government: National Industrial, Commercial, Communications, Foodstuffs, and Resources Director. This system of mercantilism, as explained earlier, where government and business work hand-in-hand to reinforce each other's power and to restrict individual freedom, is not at all related to genuine capitalism according to the Austrian School. We can see that entrenched bureaucrats' influence over business, as "career administrators," has existed for many years, while presenting a façade that they are indeed separate entities. Vonnegut narrates that "[b]usiness and bureaucracy had stuck together long enough to overwhelm the military and had since then worked side-by-side, abusively and suspiciously . . . each unable to do a whole job without the other" (*Player Piano* 84). Doctor Halyard claims that such a model has improved life for all citizens, and while that may appear true, there are still tremendous inefficiencies in this form of production when labor is employed by the government. This wastefulness is evident numerous times in the novel. Government road workers leave tools in the street and waste time throwing rocks at squirrels, standing around talking and smoking while one worker fills a hole as forty others mindlessly watch (29–31). Later, we see government workers painting useless traffic lines on the road (entirely unnecessary due to the lack of commuters), and again, lazy behavior prevails: "Three men were painting, twelve were directing traffic, and another twelve were resting" (167).

The government also designates what position each citizen will end up occupying through national standardized tests that are produced and adjudicated by machines. In the case of Bud Calhoun, we witness how inaccurate such tests can be in predicting productivity. Paul knows that Bud is a great designer, as he has already constructed important and useful machines, but Bud's university scores do not reflect his natural capabilities (Vonnegut, *Player Piano* 76). Standardized tests, as employed by a faceless government program or piece of machinery, make mistakes judging people's aptitude, particularly for creative tasks, and real world applicability is more important than laboratory knowledge. By way of humans' subjective values, capitalism pushes resources to where they are most efficient and productive through the freedom of the market, unlike the intrusive government policy of central planning, which sees statistics only as a means to increase control over individuals. The power of the government, when combined with industrial authority, presents a dangerous paternalism in which citizens no longer need to think for themselves. "The system acts like an all-powerful father," one critic of the novel writes. "The system takes over the role traditionally played by fathers in nuclear families and reduces all people, regardless of age, to the status of children. . . . The system oversimplifies human life and reinforces the idea that the industrial system is an all-good, all-powerful father for everyone" (Marvin 35–36). It is this form of paternalism, not technological progress, which inhibits creativity and obstructs people's path toward achieving a life purpose.

Donald E. Morse writes that in *Player Piano*,

> The Corporation, working to establish its notion of utopia here on earth, actively opposes any belief in the importance of variety in humans and their experience. All in the name of making everything as easy as possible for everyone and granting everyone a far greater degree of certainty than is usually possible in a non-planned, unregulated, free society. (25)

But Morse is ignoring that the business world does not create laws. While it may agree with the establishment of certain laws, no corporation is powerful enough to establish utopia; rather, the utopia derives from government policies that are working in conjunction with the corporation. After all, business cannot force a citizen to join the army; or to study certain subjects in school; or to buy a certain number of products, as alluded to in the novel. Only a totalitarian government can wield such authority, and that is the true danger portrayed in the novel—not automation, industry, or big business.

This text, while intending to show the problems with a mechanized future, ironically hinders its own argument by showing that the town of Ilium, and by extension the United States, is actually harmed most of all by a government of central planning. It is not the machines that ultimately reduce freedom, creativity, and integrity; it is the calculations of bureaucrats that stifle happiness. It is not the market or corporations that ultimately create despair; it is intrusive government that implements laws of misery. It can thus be argued that the novel is actually a criticism of government involvement in market forces. Regarding such government intrusion, it becomes difficult to discern exactly what Vonnegut's point is in this novel. He claims that employees have lost their dignity due to the lack of meaningful work, that they have lost their sense of manhood and purpose. However, in a capitalistic system, in which individuals are free to choose their employment paths and possibly to fail miserably in that choice, Vonnegut would likely also proffer complaints. So which is it? Does Vonnegut want the freedom, but uncertainty, that capitalism provides, or the perceived security, yet inevitable boredom, that government planning provides? He can't have it both ways. I have already explored the flaws with government intervention elsewhere, so let us stipulate, according the capitalist literary-critical model, that the marriage between business and government is harmful to citizen consumers. Since Vonnegut himself views automation as a fount of dystopia, sympathizing as he does with labor forces and criticizing technological advancements, we shall engage that particular vision for the remainder of this chapter and examine the effectiveness of Vonnegut's satirical presentation and his postmodernist perspective according to historical and economic principles advocated by the Austrian School.

Vonnegut's representation of American industry's demise at the hands of automation technology is rooted in classical economics. British economist David Ricardo, a predecessor of Marx, first offered his theory on the dangers of automation several decades earlier. Ricardo's 1817 work, *On the Principles of Political Economy and Taxation*, explains the labor theory of value in connection with mechanization. Ricardo writes, "I am convinced that the substitution of machinery for human labor is often very injurious to the interests of the class of laborers." He describes how an improvement in efficiency or production does not necessarily translate to an increase in value, which can, in turn, be detrimental to an economy. He also worries that while net production may increase, gross production may not, which ultimately leads to unemployment (379). Ricardo feared, ultimately, that an explosion in technology could create an economic atmosphere in which "population will become redundant, and the situation of the laborious classes will be that of distress and poverty" (381). Marx subsequently took Ricardo's ideas much further.

Vonnegut's novel makes a strong case for the detrimental effects of "alienated labor," a term Marx employed to demonstrate the separation that occurs when economic activities do not align with one's ability to express one's humanity. Humans become beholden to capitalistic processes and are no longer connected to their own self-fulfillment. As mechanization and production advance, and human labor is diminished and ultimately replaced, people become further and further estranged from their self-actualizing purpose as individual economic agents. This estrangement creates an economic structure in which humans' intelligence and physical capabilities are reduced in value, and they are eventually rendered subservient to machine. In the notes for his unfinished *Grundrisse*, Marx writes,

> The worker's activity, limited to a mere abstraction, is determined and regulated on all sides by the movement of the machinery, not the other way around. The knowledge that obliges the inanimate parts of the

machine, through their construction, to work appropriately as an automaton, does not exist in the consciousness of the worker, but acts upon him through the machine as an alien force, as the power of the machine itself. (McLellan 408–9)

Through the Shah's description of the citizen as "slave" during his tour of America, we can almost hear Vonnegut's anti-capitalist philosophy through Marx's language: "the value object defined in machinery appears as a prerequisite, opposed to which the valorizing power of the individual worker disappears" (McLellan 409). The machines cause enslavement because they work in competition with regular workers: as one character in the novel notes, "Anybody that competes with slaves becomes a slave" (Vonnegut, *Player Piano* 266). Another character adds, "People are finding that, because of the way the machines are changing the world, more and more of their old values don't apply any more. People have no choice but to become second-rate machines themselves, or wards of the machines" (274). Marx underscores this point as he writes, "Machines can only develop in opposition to living labor, as a hostile power and alien property, i.e. they must, as capital, oppose the worker" (McLellan 421). Humanity and machine are, according to Marx, in eternal conflict.

This conflict has played out in very real and violent ways during certain periods of history. The dissatisfaction of laborers with workplace conditions and, for some, the acknowledgement that their work was being replaced by machines led to uprisings in England and the formation of a resistance group called the Luddites, named after an earlier dissident, Ned Ludd. Historian Joyce Appleby explains that examples of worker rebellion—such as destroying shearing frames, spinning wheels, mole plows, threshing machines, and other nineteenth century technological advancements—were successful for a time and exceedingly common, occurring over 400 times in Great Britain alone during the century of the Industrial Revolution. However, workers eventually accepted that machines were not going anywhere and resorted to other forms of resistance, such as unionization and labor negotiation to address their concerns (Appleby 152–54). But, for anti-capitalists, the struggle between human and machine continues.

Those economists from the Austrian School, however, bring a decidedly different perspective to the question of mechanization and employment. Mises says, "The Ricardo effect is by and large stock-in-trade of popular economics. Nonetheless, the theorem involved is one of the worst economic fallacies. The confusion starts with the misinterpretation of the statement that machinery is 'substituted' for labor." He explains that technological improvements are not designed and implemented as a means to reduce labor, but rather to increase production. If there were no potential for production efficiency, then technology would not be adopted. By maximizing efficiency in the production process, entirely new projects may then be undertaken that were previously unfeasible due to unfilled consumer demand. With more supply at hand, more consumption and, ultimately, more leisure time are possible, in turn opening up new kinds of demand, new kinds of production, and new kinds of employment. What those goods will be and how leisure is enjoyed is up to the individual, subjective values of the consumers. Understanding this relationship, Mises writes, "explodes all talk about 'technological unemployment'" (*Human Action* 768).

The goal of an individual business, on a microeconomic level, or of a national economy, on a macro scale, is not to create jobs. The goal of all economic endeavors is create *wealth*, that is, subjective value, for all involved—owners, employees, consumers, investors, and anyone else directly or indirectly affiliated. Jobs are not ends. It is only the accumulation of capital through effective production that creates jobs both now and in the future. Capital is the end goal. Jobs are the means, and, circularly, only exist by way of capital. Capital can exist without jobs; jobs cannot exist without capital. Therefore, hindering access to capital leads to a stagnation of job growth. We must remember that "[m]odern industrialism was not intent upon designedly increasing the joy of labor"—or even the amount of available labor. "It relied," Mises writes, "upon the material improvement that it brought to the employees in their capacity as wage earners as well as in their capacity as consumers and buyers of the products" (*Human Action* 587). The number of jobs in an economy is not a signal of prosperity. Large nations such as the Soviet Union, India, and China have always had more access to labor, but they have always been poorer than the United States. Even those living in poverty in America tend to be richer than many who live in those other countries, and this is arguably because Americans have tended to create more economic wealth. Not much good comes from having a supposedly low-level, steady job while starving to death. On the other hand, having a low-level or blue-collar job can provide a very comfortable lifestyle in America. Mises writes,

> The substitution of more efficient methods of production for less efficient ones does not render labor abundant. . . . On the contrary, it increases output and thereby the quantity of consumers' goods. "Laborsaving" devices reduce want. They do not bring about "technological unemployment." Every product is the result of the employment both of labor and of material factors. Man economizes both labor and material factors. (*Human Action* 136–37)

The economist, journalist, and literary critic Henry Hazlitt, who follows in the Austrian tradition, also argues against the concept of technological unemployment:

Among the most viable of all economic delusions is the belief that machines on net balance create unemployment. The belief that all machines cause unemployment, when held with any logical consistency, leads to preposterous conclusions. Not only must we be causing unemployment with every technological improvement we make today, but primitive man must have started causing it with the first efforts he made to save himself from needless toil and sweat. (*Economics* 49)

Hazlitt recounts how the stocking industry during the Industrial Revolution actually *increased* employment after improving technology and machinery. The same effect occurred later with textile production as well (50). The unwarranted fear of advancing technology ultimately leads to unwarranted labor regulations and unionization in an attempt to maintain power in bureaucratic hands (52–53). This pattern occurs in the novel not only in business, but also in government, demonstrating that the increased production-stifling regulation is not solely imposed upon the private sector. Hazlitt remarks further that even supposedly smart people are duped by this fallacy, such as Nobel Prize winner Gunnar Myrdal in his book, *The Challenge of World Poverty.* "His book opposed the introduction of labor-saving machines in the underdeveloped countries on the ground that they 'decrease the demand for labor!'" Hazlitt writes. "The logical conclusion from this would be that the way to maximize jobs is to make all labor as inefficient and unproductive as possible" (53). Our new era is no different than any other time, but opponents of machinery will claim it is. Hazlitt notes how Eleanor Roosevelt once wrote in a 1945 newspaper column, "We have reached a point today where labor-saving devices are good only when they do not throw the worker out of his job." If this were true, everything humans have ever done or ever will do to be more efficient in labor would have to be considered potentially disastrous. The eternal struggle humanity faces is the attempt to reduce labor while achieving desirable results. Economic efficiency is always, and always has been, the ultimate goal. "The technophobes, if they were logical and consistent," Hazlitt says, "would have to dismiss all this progress and ingenuity as not only useless but vicious. Why should freight be carried from Chicago to New York by railroad when we could employ enormously more men, for example, to carry it all on their backs?" (54).

The premise that technological innovation displaces human labor, thus increasing unemployment, is not only inaccurate economically, but it has shown to be false. Historical data, contemporaneous to Vonnegut's time of writing *Player Piano* underscores this. In 1963, University of Chicago economist Yale Brozen wrote, "Since 1940, production worker employment in manufacturing has increased by 52 percent while [that of] other workers increased by over 100 percent." There is very little evidence for a correlation between technological advancement and unemployment. "The primary effect of automation," Brozen writes, "is not a reduction in the number of jobs available. Rather, it makes it possible for us to do many things which otherwise could not and would not be done" (7). President John F. Kennedy once warned the American people that roughly 1.8 million people per year lose their jobs to machines. However, Brozen points out, that frightening statistic does not quite fit with the evidence: "Presumably, 18 million persons lost their jobs in the 1950s because of machines; yet, total employment rose by seven million." In other words, in the decade of Vonnegut's panic over technology, seven million *more* people were working ten years later, apparently due to the growth of national capital and increases in levels of education (8–9). A. J. Jaffe, from Columbia University, and Joseph Froomkin, a government economist, wrote in a 1968 study on automation and employment that despite the increase in post-war mechanization, unemployment was lower than previous points in the early twentieth century. "The Marxist theory that unemployment increases secularly under capitalism," they concluded, "has not been validated by the U.S. experience. . . . There is no reason to believe that technological change causes unemployment" (69). Technology helps to create jobs and improve our lifestyles; this was true in Vonnegut's era and continues still.

Player Piano also offers some support to the Austrian perspective on this point. What is discussed throughout the novel, and parallel to real-world economics, is that this wealth is due to increased production, but not to more manual labor. We see that Ilium has been transformed into a place where jobs could be done "more quickly and efficiently and cheaply by machines" (Vonnegut, *Player Piano* 10). Paul bemoans the human error and inefficiency that existed before the development of automation:

> The lathes were of the old type, built originally to be controlled by men, and adapted during the war, clumsily, to the new techniques. The accuracy was going out of them, and, as the meter in Katharine's office had pointed out, rejects were showing up in quantity. Paul was willing to bet that the lathe group was 10 percent as wasteful as it had been in the days of human control and mountainous scrap heaps. (17)

Paul wonders how industry survived in the days before automation. He notes how expensive, unreliable, and wasteful the factories must have been as "every kind of human trouble is likely to show up in a product one way or another" (22). Even the bright Bud Calhoun acknowledges that one of his creations is an improvement over his own human labor: "Does [the job] a whole lot better than Ah did it" (75). Ultimately, it must be admitted that "machines were doing America's work far better than Americans ever done it. There were better goods for more people at less cost, and who could deny that that was magnificent and gratifying?" (56).

Eventually, however, Paul feels guilty about the success of automated industry, seemingly at the expense of the displaced laborers. He tells his wife, "In order to get what we've got, Anita, we have, in effect, traded these people out of what was the most important thing on earth to them—the feeling of being needed and useful, the foundation of self-respect" (Vonnegut, *Player Piano* 169). He wants her to have a sense of what their "way of life has done to the lives of others" (170). This zero-sum way of thinking about economics is at the heart of the anti-capitalist philosophy, and ignores the effects of production on widespread prosperity. Economist Thomas Sowell reminds us that if exploitation of labor were true, we would see places with exceptional wealth juxtaposed with disastrous poverty. For example, since the United States leads the world in billionaires, we would also have to lead the world in poverty among the working class. However, America has long been the envy of the world regarding standard of living for average, working citizens. On the other hand, other nations in the world with extreme poverty among laborers have very few extremely wealthy citizens. The exploitation theory is simply incorrect (Sowell, *Basic Economics* 252). And we need to look no further than the average citizens of Ilium to see how prosperous they actually are. Starvation and violence have practically disappeared. Everyone has access to the latest household products. And when manual labor still needs to be done, it is not nearly as strenuous as it once was. While there are still levels of wealth in Ilium, as indicated by the three sections of town described in the novel's opening paragraph, no one is particularly poor. Contrast Ilium with anywhere else in the world—either in the novel's timeline or in our own—and we would have to agree that it is an astonishingly prosperous place.

Machinery, some say, takes away jobs from humans, which hinders their ability to survive; but some also believe it reduces something else that work provides people—integrity and personal satisfaction. One critic agrees with the cultural backlash against automation as he describes the dreary town of Ilium:

> Here there is no dignity in labor, no virtue in an "honest day's wages," no reward for exceeding expectations. Instead, people realize that the corporate world wishes to use their labor as cheaply as possible and will replace them with more reliable machines whenever and wherever possible, not stopping to count or even acknowledge the human cost of those dismissed, fired, or forced to quit. (Morse 26)

Capitalism's demand for production ignores the desires of humanity, as this form of "electronically run society places the good of the corporation and the *full employment of machines* ahead of human needs and desires, including the human necessity for meaningful work" (Morse 27; original emphasis). At numerous points throughout the novel, characters feel as if a part of themselves, a piece of their human potential, is either underutilized or completely missing. Paul fantasizes about living in colonial times with immense amounts of labor required just to survive (Vonnegut, *Player Piano* 110). He eventually begins to feel more rebellious and adventurous, reading books about free, outdoor living and romanticizing a heroic, vigorous life: "there is a basic truth underlying the tales, a primitive ideal to which he could aspire. He wanted to deal, not with society, but only with Earth as God had given it to man" (135). One woman who meets the visiting Shah takes pleasure in her broken washing machine, that she is happy to do the work (160). And, of course, Bud Calhoun is presented as the novel's happiest man, mostly because he works with his hands and enjoys his manual labor of gadgeteering. The satisfaction found in challenging labor is offered as indicative of our humanity, that it is in the daily struggle for subsistence and purpose that we find pleasure. It is in the automated society that we forget how to enjoy life, how to be humans, as Vonnegut argues that "Human beings exist to make things, to be of use or produce something useful, thereby expressing a reason for being" (Klinkowitz 44).

Technological advancement, therefore, does not necessarily correlate with our hope that life will automatically tend toward improvement. It is with this pessimistic perspective that many critics choose to support Vonnegut's thematic implications: "The master narrative of *Player Piano* is a myth, to America and often reified in the genre of utopian science-fiction: mechanical progress means a better future for all" (Davis 42). This novel is not futuristic in its presentation, but rather "describes the logical consequences of social forces already apparent in the 1950s," one of which being "an uncritical faith in technology and 'progress'" (Marvin 25–26). The tragic irony, one critic notes, is that "The inventiveness that provides so many Americans with their principal joy in life may eventually make them obsolete" (33). The danger that Vonnegut warns us against lies in what he sees as humanity's reluctance to realize the long-term and systemic effects of achieving success in industrial automation— ultimately, unemployment and unhappiness.

The foundation of any discussion on the role of automation on production, however, has to do with the very definition of labor, primarily that it is inherently a form of disutility, or, in other words, is itself a form of adversity. Mises reminds us that "the real world is conditioned by the disutility of labor. Only theorems based on the assumption that labor is a source of uneasiness are applicable for the comprehension of what is going on in this world" (*Human Action* 65). By contrast, much of *Player Piano* offers characters that feel unfulfilled because they are not laboring in endeavors they love. In other words, they claim to enjoy and receive dignity from their jobs. However, since humans always act in an effort to remove uneasiness, according to definitions of labor, if we truly love our work, we would never cease working because the received joy would outweigh other options of pleasure. Concurrently, we would not tend to want to consume, which is the ultimate purpose of production in the first place. Furthermore, if we truly loved work, we would automatically do it for free. Therefore, labor or work, by definition, is an attempt to do something we dislike in an effort to achieve something we enjoy more at a later time, usually through the attainment of money or some other benefit. This is not to say that we cannot enjoy our jobs, but we always demand payment, which implies that we will use that payment to achieve an increase of happiness at a future time that is inherently worth more than our current laborious condition. The only way to attain the means for happiness is to do things that we find unhappy. This is the tradeoff that leads to consumption of other activities. As an example, we may love the activity of university teaching. However, if we truly received ultimate satisfaction from that work, we would never leave the office or the class-room, because it would only be while at work that we achieve happiness. Additionally, we would gladly show up to school for free, because, again, our pleasure outweighs the need to obtain any other form of happiness.

On the contrary, we work so that we may eat, put shelter over our heads, keep children healthy, go on vacation, attend sporting events and concerts, buy new televisions, and the like. We inherently value those things more because that is what we *set aside work for*. By definition, then, work is less valuable to us than myriad other activities. We only do it to purchase other forms of happiness. Vonnegut's hope that we should en-joy our labor for labor's sake and to be part of an integrated social fabric simply does not fit, as Mises notes, with the realities of economics:

> In our actual world things are different. The expenditure of labor is deemed painful. Not to work is considered a state of affairs more satis-factory than working. Leisure is, other things being equal, preferred to travail. People work only when they value the return of labor higher than the decrease in satisfaction brought about by the curtailment of leisure. To work involves disutility. (*Human Action* 131–32)

Humans prefer non-work to work, despite the hopes of classical econo-mists, and the accessibility of non-work is most available to the most amount of people (including the working classes) in a capitalistic econo-my. Marx disagrees, as he writes, "The creation of nonworking time is, from the capitalist standpoint, and from that of all earlier stages of devel-opment, nonworking time or free time for the few" (McLellan 416). But this line of thinking has things backward. Working time is non-free time, and this is true for all. It is not just the wealthy few that benefit from capitalism's increased efficiency. *Everyone* in the free-market economy ultimately enjoys such improvements in some form or another.

An argument can be made that work is linked to happiness. Studies do report that those unemployed, or without work, are less happy than those with opportunities for work. However, this may be just another way of saying that unemployment has led to some form of material need, if not outright poverty. Certainly, deprivation is a more reasonable cause of unhappiness than simply not being able to go to work. In Vonnegut's fictional town of Ilium, though, material need is not a factor, because everyone is provided a stable and generous income through government subsidy. Therefore, while we may concede that part of humanity enjoys participating in a functionally useful role, either through employment or elsewhere, we cannot conclusively infer that it is work, in itself, that creates a positive sense of providing an increase in use value. When given the option between work and leisure, people overwhelmingly tend to choose leisure and avoid work. According to one study, even when the possibility of promotion or an increased salary is offered, workers opt for more free time instead (Rifkin 233). And even in a great job that provides autonomy and creativity, or a position in which we volunteer or serve without remuneration, we nonetheless do less of it than we choose to have leisure because it is still labor, still a disutility, despite being enjoyable. This all prompts an important question: if we love work so much, as Vonnegut claims, then why do laborers and unions constantly battle for fewer working hours? If workers loved work so much, they would do more of it. But that is simply not what the data suggest. Family, travel, exercise, entertainment, rest, and other options for leisure tend to win out because we gain more satisfaction from them than we do from work. More free time, and leisure availability, is what mechanization and technological advancement has always provided and will continue to do so.

Economists Mark Aguiar and Erik Hurst find that *all* working-age Americans have gained more leisure time in the last forty years. Even women, who have entered the labor force at a higher rate and work more hours than they did in the 1960s and 1970s, have actually enjoyed more leisure time as well. Furthermore, very counter-intuitively for the anti-capitalist point of view, those with lower education and skills seem to have benefited the most over this period of time, as they enjoy more free time than their more-educated, higher-skilled counterparts. This fact is often neglected in the debate over income inequality, as those earning more money tend to work significantly more hours than those who earn less. The trade-off, however, is that though lower earners accumulate less income, they have more leisure time available. Income inequality is actually an inevitable inverse of "leisure inequality." The result is that females and lower-skilled workers especially have enjoyed and continue to enjoy substantial benefits from industrial increases in efficiency and productivity. This information suggests a significant rise in the standard of living and quality of life for the average citizen in particular. Compared even to the recent mid-twentieth century portrayed in Vonnegut's novel, Americans have gained considerably more access to their own pleasures and pursuits than that enjoyed by of previous generations.

In his work *Singularity Rising*, economist and technology expert James D. Miller offers a glimpse of what the technological possibilities for the future may hold. There is a distinct opportunity before us that technological improvements will continue to compound and humanity will continue to benefit with increasing speed and efficiency. "In the past, job-destroying machine production has overall greatly benefited workers,"

Miller writes. "'Destroying jobs' sounds bad—like something that should harm an economy. But the benefits of job destruction become apparent when you realize that an economy's most valuable resource is human brains" (131). The more our brains are employed in creative and enterprising activities, and less in menial and backbreaking labor, the more our lives and the world's economies improve. This has already happened with American agriculture, Miller writes:

> The obliteration of most agricultural jobs has been a huge source of economic growth for America. In 1900, farmers made up 38 percent of the American workforce, whereas now they constitute less than two percent of it. . . . Yet despite the massive decrease in farming jobs, the United States has steadily produced more and more food since 1900. Agricultural technology gave the American people . . . more food with less effort, making obesity a greater threat to American health than calorie deprivation. (132)

The automation that has enhanced our lives exponentially over the last 150 years will surge forward until, at some point, machines might do almost all of our work and we might spend almost all of our time in leisure. Even a pro-labor advocate like economist and activist Jeremy Rifkin agrees that technology may replace the necessity for human work as early as the twenty-second century. This would allow nearly everyone to pursue personal pleasure, education, and culture more enthusiastically and to produce much more original value for their communities. "After all," Rifkin writes, "work should be what machines do." And freeing people from drudgery in favor of a more creative "civil society represents a great potential leap forward for humanity in the coming century" (xli). Through the continuing improvement of intelligent technology, our future holds the possibility for a very real and not-too-distant form of utopia.

One of the most fascinating parts of *Player Piano* is the corporate retreat, where the engineers and business owners have bonding exercises and put on skits to reinforce their commitment to industrial management. This section of the text is intended to satirize the corporatists for their utilitarian dedication to increased production and its subsequent improvements in standard of living. One actor, playing the role of a humble, low-level employee, says, "It hurts a lot to be forgotten. You know—to have the fellers in charge, the engineers and managers, just sort of look right through him like they don't see him. A guy likes to know somebody thinks enough of him to look out for him" (Vonnegut, *Player Piano* 205). Another actor, as an engineer, replies that even though pay might have slightly decreased, the standard of living—for everyone—has increased dramatically. What was once reserved only for the wealthy is now available to the commoner (207). He continues to explain that the bosses actually work *for* the employees, as nothing is possible without employees and consumers being satisfied. And their high pay is compensation for start-up costs in which employees had to be paid from the start (208). While this is meant to poke fun at capitalism's apparent apathy and inherent unfairness, and at how it is reified in the hearts and minds of current and future corporate leaders, one salient aspect of this satirical presentation must not be ignored: it is largely true. The industrial and technological ages have improved everyone's lives enormously. Satisfaction of consumers is what makes a market economy function, and the ability to maintain production (either from employees or machines) is what sustains that economy. And start-up costs in which materials and risk must be accounted for, as well as payment of employees or other forms of capital investment, are all incurred before the business owner ever earns a single dollar. The entrepreneur is *last* on the chain of payment, if there is any remaining profit, while also remaining fully responsible for covering any loss. Vonnegut's aim at discrediting such a benevolent system is undermined somewhat by his own contradictory portrayals, and certainly by the empirical evidence that confronts us daily. Mocking an economic philosophy that has undoubtedly made the world a better place is a rather daring endeavor.

Vonnegut's avowed aims in writing the novel provide even further insight into the flaws of the anti-capitalist position. In an interview years after the release of the book, Vonnegut said that evolving technology as an improvement to the workplace "made sense, perfect sense. To have a little clicking box make all the decisions wasn't a vicious thing to do. But it was too bad for the human beings who got their dignity from their jobs" (Standish 93). Vonnegut's admission here skewers the anti-capitalist perspective, both in economics and in literary criticism. Despite recognizing that technological innovation and its resulting engineering efficiency was the logical progression for an industrial nation, and that such a progression was not the insidious master scheme of some reviled corporatist, but rather a natural evolution of improved manufacturing methods, Vonnegut confesses that it was not a safer and cheaper manufacturing process he really wanted, whereby all citizens could raise their standard of living by less expensive production and more valuable purchasing power, but that he simply *felt bad* for the laborer. This emphasis on an emotional connection, rather than on logical argumentation, typifies the anti-capitalist methodology. Regardless of the many advances capitalism has brought forth into the world, this economic process is still liable to be denigrated by anti-capitalists if a common worker must adapt to the changing environment by finding a more useful line of employment.

The ideas of Ricardo, Marx, and Vonnegut actually still exist today—and among very powerful people. In a 2011 interview in which he addressed the issue of sustained unemployment, President Barack Obama stated, "There are some structural issues with our economy where a lot of businesses have learned to become much more efficient with a lot fewer workers. You see it when you go to a bank and you use an ATM, you don't go to a bank teller, or you go to the airport and you're using a kiosk instead of checking in at the gate." In this specific case, and in much discussion about technology in general, it is clear that the president has elided the additional labor required for the innovation, construction, installation, and preservation of these machines. ATMs did not arrive out of thin air—laborers made them come into existence. It also does not further the president's case that the number of bank teller jobs has dramatically *increased* since the development of ATMs. The fact remains that ATMs and other technological advancements make our lives better. We like having access to our bank accounts twenty-four hours a day, we like not having to stand in lines, and we like the improved personal control over our financial needs (Bartash). Even if employment is affected in the short term, we as consumers *prefer* technology.

Mises exposed many years ago the one-sided situation where the authors and critics who uphold this narrow viewpoint on "capitalistic industry are praised at universities as the greatest philosophers and benefactors of mankind and their teachings are accepted with reverential awe by the millions whose homes, besides other gadgets, are equipped with radio and television sets" (*The Anti-Capitalistic Mentality* 42). It should come as no surprise that Vonnegut himself cashed in on technology and market capitalism during his life while denouncing their virtues. "Vonnegut's fiction is both intellectual and proletarian in that it has attracted the attention and admiration of scholars and laborers alike," one critic writes. "In a profession where sales measure success, his publishers report that his books are selling one million hardcover and five million paperback copies per year" (Hoffman 11). Surely, his fear of technology must have subsided while he was publishing so prolifically, profiting substantially from contemporary advances in automated and highly efficient machine printing, targeted media marketing, and ubiquitous distribution channels. Apparently, machinery and the capitalistic process worked pretty well for him.

Writing in 1959, shortly after the publication of *Player Piano* and in the midst of the automation debates, Austrian School economist Murray Rothbard called for the truth about the evolution of technology to prevail: "Let us, therefore, put aside the old Luddite (machine-wrecking) bogey of technological unemployment, and hail modern developments of automation for what it is and will be: a superb method of greatly increasing the standards of living and the leisure hours, of all of us" (*Science, Technology, and Government* 30). Despite his own contrary intentions, Vonnegut's main message in *Player Piano* is that the machines we invent should lead us to more freedom, rather than enslavement. Machines should be the means to human achievement, not the ends themselves. This is something upon which both capitalists and anti-capitalists likely agree. However, the same must also be said about labor, that it is a means and not an end; and this is where capitalists and anti-capitalists tend to differ. Mises reminds us that "anti-capitalist propaganda is a systematic scheme for the substitution of tedium for the joy of labor" (*Human Action* 587–88). Labor is something we use to lead us to happiness; thus we should not elevate labor to a higher moral plane or to ultimate happiness in itself. Enjoying our labor is simply a *bonus*, not the *reason* why we work. It, too, is a means to an end, not an end itself. As a young man, Vonnegut participated in World War II, and was taken as a prisoner of war by the Germans. So if anyone should be wary of German beliefs about labor, it should be Vonnegut; after all, one scarcely needs to look further than the sign that hung above the entrance to the Auschwitz concentration camp to see what placing an undue importance on the humanizing of labor can lead to: *Arbeit Macht Frei* ("Work makes one free").

An Austrian economic reading of *Player Piano* allows the reader to penetrate Vonnegut's anti-capitalist portrayal of technology and its effects. I have argued that the root of the dystopia of *Player Piano* is not the replacement of labor by machinery, but rather in the excessive government regulation of labor and an illogical wariness about productive technology. The kinds of machinery portrayed in the novel truly do improve the material conditions of the town's citizens. The progress that is actually dangerous in the novel is political progress—when the local and national government embrace technology to the point where business and government are one and the same. But this is not an indictment of technology or business. This is an indictment of interventionist politics. Traditional economic readings of this novel have heretofore accepted unsubstantiated premises regarding the relationship between human purpose and labor. The Austrian School of capitalist literary criticism, alternatively, not only clarifies these errors of economic thinking, but also subverts Vonnegut's pessimistic and fearful vision of our nation's industrial future in terms that Vonnegut as an author, and as another kind of economic agent, did himself support.

Conclusion

The artistic and critical vision of capitalism has been ill-defined and misrepresented for far too long in literary studies. What often passes for insightful cultural criticism could be more accurately described as fearmongering, laying the difficulties of the world at the feet of a bogeyman that, I argue, serves as a convenient stand-in for the inherent complications and inadequacies of human nature. The author of the final case study examined in this book, Kurt Vonnegut, offers a searing interpretation of capitalism:

> Industries should be allowed to do whatever they want to do: bribe, wreck the environment just a little, fix prices, screw dumb customers, put a stop to competition, and raid the Treasury when they go broke.
> That's correct.
> That's free enterprise.
> And that's correct. The poor have done something very wrong or they wouldn't be poor, so their children should pay the consequences.
> That's correct.
> The United States of America cannot be expected to look after its own people.
> That's correct.
> The free market will do that.
> That's correct.
> The free market is an automatic system of justice.
> That's correct.
> I'm kidding. (*A Man Without A Country* 84–85)

Though his last sentence attempts to ease the tension behind his harsh views, Vonnegut is most certainly not kidding about his feelings of capitalism. And this perspective is by no means unique to the often-eccentric Vonnegut. This reductive and hostile understanding of economic processes unfortunately characterizes much of what passes for economics-oriented literary criticism.

The distaste for capitalism in literary criticism may be mirrored by many economists, particularly those with a collectivist mindset. Hayek's biographer writes, "Hayek was defeated by Keynes in the economic debates of the 1930s, not, I think, because Keynes 'proved' his point, but because, once the world economy had collapsed, no one was very interested in the question of what exactly had caused it" (qtd. in Wapshott 285). The same could be said of the hopeful power of anti-capitalist messages throughout English studies. Like literary criticism, which reflects many critics' own beliefs about what literature can or should be, much of economic theory is adopted based not on factual evidence or axiomatic truths of human behavior, but on hope, optimism, and feelings that elicit positivity toward future conditions. Though many of Keynes's ideas were later proven wrong, people loved his ideas more because they *sounded hopeful.* Keynes's policy suggestions, still embraced today by those with collectivist tendencies, could be explained away as nothing more than "errors of optimism," as if to say that failures in theory are acceptable as long as their intentions are right (189). It is easy to criticize humanity and proffer alternatives because no matter how absurd such notions may turn out to be, the high ground has been won. Truth is often a downer. The underdog wins every time in the hearts of literary critics and political economists alike. And those that are not as aware of such ramifications follow lock-step for fear of being labeled as uncaring or, worse, oppressive. The cycle is perpetuated indefinitely of questionable arguments for economics, literature, and economics in literature.

Literary critics who stand with an anti-capitalist ideology reside in a world of theory while ignoring the epistemological foundation that theory should be inherently applicable to the functioning world. They do this because they either have no concrete knowledge of real-world conditions and theorizing social visions is their default setting; or, it is simply easier to live on the side of the angels. After all, posing as a defender of the oppressed can never be wrong. Actually understanding how oppression occurs and what to do to stop it seem to be mere formalities. It is the belief in the theory that matters, not the evidence required to support such a belief. Renowned historian Paul Johnson once said, "The study of history is a powerful antidote to contemporary arrogance. It is humbling to discover how many of our glib assumptions, which seem to us novel and plausible, have been tested before, not once but many times and in innumerable guises; and discovered to be, at great human cost, wholly false" (qtd. in Sowell, *Intellectuals* 281). And so critics, and professors, and students shout into the echo chamber to, perhaps, feel good about themselves, ignoring evidence from history and economics, because those who return their call feel the same way.

John Carey explains the unfortunate approach to the production and evaluation of literature that many acclaimed philosophers, authors, and critics have taken. Nietzsche wrote, "That everyone can learn to read will ruin in the long run not only writing, but thinking too." D. H. Lawrence added, "The great mass of humanity should never learn to read or write." T. S. Eliot believed that there had been "too many books published," and such an expansion of literacy had been "one of the evil effects of democracy." And Aldous Huxley claimed that literacy and education had "created an immense class of what I may call the New Stupid" (qtd. in *The Intellectuals* 15–16). Among the authors discussed in this book, Kurt

Vonnegut also ignores the authority of reader, instead privileging himself. Vonnegut once stated, "I think writers are the most important members of society, not just potentially but actually" (Bellamy and Casey 166). I believe, instead, readers are the most important members. Just like consumers, we determine the success of the producers. An author's ideas go nowhere if the readers disregard them, just as a new product fails in the marketplace if consumers ignore it. Vonnegut's view is that of the greedy businessman, proclaiming more importance for himself than is properly due. The best business owners are those that realize they must satisfy or at least provide some function for the consumer through creativity and innovation. Readers are society's most important entity, holding the power to choose to accept new ideas and change a culture. Otherwise, like one shouting into outer space, an author may offer a voice but no resonating sound. The act of reading is economically powerful according to the capitalist model.

It is sadly ironic that a nation with such a rich tradition of individualism in literature—Thoreau's "Civil Disobedience" and Emerson's "Self-Reliance" come to mind, as do Twain's Huck Finn, Rand's Howard Roark, Cather's Alexandra Bergson, and Kesey's Hank Stamper and Randall MacMurphy—has promoted literary criticism that is overwhelmingly dominated by notions of collectivism and group identification. Through anti-capitalist methodologies we have become a nation of conformists, artistically and critically. "As a doctrine that undermines the idea of individual human agency," Paul Cantor writes, "Marxism seems inappropriate to the study of art—a realm often taken to be the highest form of human self-expression, creativity, and freedom" (17). This perpetuation inevitably creates dullness. "The greatest danger, in short, of so-called Marxian criticism in literature," Henry Hazlitt writes, "is that the critics who make a fetish or a cult of it will in time become infinitely boring." I believe those who surround themselves with creativity, like literature critics and teachers, yearn for something more. And it is always the new and exciting individual, not the vague and faceless class structures and cultural constructions, whic we remember. Hazlitt reminds us that identifying a particular author as upper-class is as uninteresting as saying "that Rousseau was an eighteenth-century writer, that Goethe was a German, and that atheists are not Catholics." Rather, we should focus on what distinguishes an author's individuality, "in brief, what makes him still worth talking about at all" (*The Anatomy* 286).

The ultimate beauty of literature is that it may exist for the simultaneous pleasure of two diametrically opposing perspectives. While I think Richard Wright's tale of Bigger Thomas is historically misleading and economically uninformed, I receive tremendous pleasure from the boy's struggles to create an identity for himself and his seeking reconciliation for his violent acts. I harbor the same conflicted feelings about Vonnegut's portrayal of industrial America. However, each book achieves its purpose at its most basic premise: it brings some degree of pleasure to the reader. And while I may not pursue the same critical interpretations as more traditional theorists in today's academia, our joy in the work *as a piece of work* may be mutual. Likewise, there will surely be critics who disagree with my interpretation of Douglass's autobiography and will claim that I still do not understand, on an emotional level, the historic plight of either slaves or present-day African Americans. Nevertheless, those critics and I may still share the intensity of a harrowing journey of an escaped slave and enjoy the pleasure of reading the words of a man that, by their very existence, are miraculous and worthy of praise. If art exists, as its most rudimentary function, to display humanity in an enlightening and enjoyable fashion, then there will always be, even during the most heated of debates among critics, a junction at which we may and must agree.

Bear in mind that my economic analysis does not promote a claim to how "good" a text may be. I do not state that *Native Son* or *The Grapes of Wrath*, for example, are "bad" works of literature. In fact, I feel quite the opposite. We may ultimately say what I. A. Richards once said: "I don't like this, but I know it is good" (Hazlitt, *The Anatomy* 90). Nor do I state that because of my style of analysis, Douglass's *Narrative* should be interpreted as especially "good" literature. Rather, I believe it was good long before I ever analyzed it. Therefore, my analysis is not an indictment of the success of the literature as a piece of art. My analysis critiques the effectiveness of that art's representation as well as the validity of criticisms of that art by way of a capitalist methodology.

A capitalist criticism reinvigorates the conversation about authorial creativity and literary characters. And this perspective should be embraced. F. A. Hayek reminds us that under various historical circumstances, "No reproach was more feared or more fatal to academic prospects than that of being an 'apologist' of the capitalist system; and, even if a scholar dared to contradict dominant opinion on a particular point, he would be careful to safeguard himself against such accusation by joining in the general condemnation of the capitalist system" (*Capitalism and the Historians* 23). But academia is no different today. Professors and critics defend the anti-capitalist position, forgetting the fact that it is the same capitalist system that allows them to take such a position and succeed from it. In the spirit of Marxist study as a form of rebellion against pervasive capitalist ideologies, the Austrian economic perspective is likewise a rebellion against pervasive anti-capitalist ideologies which dominate Humanities departments at nearly all levels of universities. In an ironic twist of cultural history, anti-capitalists are mainstream; today, capitalists are the rebels. Siding with the "oppressed" carries much less weight when those that feel oppressed are actually the ones in authority.

Collectivist principles may have once worked, and anthropological evidence has proven it, in households and small villages where everyone was able to hold one another accountable. In such enclaves, sharing re-sources was the norm because greed and selfishness were held in check by the other members of the family or group. But as societies developed into cities and nations, markets (and specifically the pricing mechanism) became the most efficient way to connect personal responsibility to free transactions with others based on want and need. If the claim that capi-talists (often politically termed "conservatives") are living in the past is actually true, and the only form of collectivism that has ever worked is thousands of years old, one may deduce that the most "conservative" people on the planet are actually today's leftists, Marxists, and progres-sives.

Not only does capitalism need a reintroduction to the academy and the literary world at large, but as what may be the most enlightening, hopeful, accurate, uplifting, peaceful, and pragmatic philosophy the world has ever known. Hayek writes,

> We must clear away the rubble that has accumulated on this ancient citadel since Marx and Engels wrote. And the rubble is so heavy: di-alectical revolution, rationalistic spirit, human exploitation, personal greed—all the cant, fury, and misguided sentiment of 100 years! The digging is worth our efforts, for at the bottom we shall find a system and a set of attitudes just made possible material progress and the alleviation of human suffering. (*Capitalism and the Historians* 75)

And we should embrace such a debate. One man who was an intimate participant in the philosophical and economic debates between F. A. Hayek and J. M. Keynes in the 1930s, Cambridge economist Austin Rob-inson, once said, "It is only by argument, by conflict if you like, that economics makes progress" (qtd. in Wapshott 67). The same is true for literary criticism. The only way to advance literary studies is by challeng-ing the prevailing models. The future of political and cultural advance-ment may very well depend on the acknowledgement of a new form of artistic interpretation, and specifically literary criticism. And the literary field itself will be better off for it.

In his excellent book *The Wisdom of Crowds*, business writer James Surowiecki explains how groups do not become more intelligent or in-sightful by continuously borrowing from one another. Rather, the group, as a whole, becomes wiser by its participants working largely as individ-uals. He writes, "The more influence we exert on each other, the more likely it is that we will believe the same things and make the same mis-takes. That means it's possible that we could become individually smart-er but collectively dumber" (42). In literary criticism, if the vast majority of critics think similarly in applying economic forms of analysis, the like-lihood increases that faulty theory may prevail. Surowiecki calls this the "information cascade dilemma." He writes,

> The information cascade is not always the result of mindless trend-following, or conformity, or peer pressure. . . . People fall in line because they believe they're learning something important from the example of others . . . and this is perfectly logical. . . . However, the fundamental problem with an information cascade is that after a certain point it becomes rational for people to stop paying attention to their own knowledge—their private information—and to start looking instead to the actions of others and imitate them. Thus, the cascade stops becoming informative. Everyone thinks that people are making decisions based on what they know, when in fact people are making decisions based on what they think the people who came before them knew. (54–55)

In literary studies, by continuing the trend of anti-capitalist economic criticism, and simply following along with what has come before, many critics seem to have fallen into the trap of assuming everything previous is a hard and fast rule, rather than something to be legitimately debated. The role of the individual analyst, in presenting an alternative perspective, will actually strengthen the entire group's integrity.

Surowiecki notes that the more important the debate, the less likely an information cascade will occur, which is positive because it indicates that people will increasingly arrive at more valid results when they are needed most (63). Conversely, however, logic follows that since literary criticism is not exactly near the top of the list of world problems to be solved, the likelihood of information cascade increases. This is clearly indicated throughout the existing history of our field. Surowiecki urges us to take an alternate path: "One key to successful group decisions is getting people to pay much less attention to what everyone else is saying" (65). I hope that I have demonstrated throughout this book Paul Cantor's distinction between two economic literary criticisms: "One of the differences between Austrian economics and Marxism," he writes, "is that it does not present itself as a master science, with an underlying explanation for all phenomena. Thus our reliance on Austrian economics allows us to avoid the reductionist tendencies of readings of literature that are rooted in Marxist assumptions" (xvi).

An Austrian economic perspective presents a new and independent way of approaching literary criticism that breaks sharply from the accepted methodology (and ideology) in an effort to find not only a more balanced form of criticism, but perhaps even a better form of criticism. Russell Berman writes that perhaps revisiting and more clearly understanding the nature of capitalism and its relationship to literature can help to assay some of its historically censured associations:

> The cultivation of imagination as the capacity to posit alternatives to the historical conditions of material scarcity and the habits of judgment and taste, which are inextricably tied up with literature, disseminate value structures and mental habits that have important ramifications

Killian, Lewis M. *White Southerners*. Amherst: University of Massachusetts Press, 1985. Print.

Kirzner, Israel. *Discovery and the Capitalist Process*. Chicago: University of Chicago Press, 1985. Print.

Klinkowitz, Jerome. *The Vonnegut Effect*. Columbia: University of South Carolina Press, 2004. Print.

Krugman, Paul. "The Humbug Express." *New York Times* 23 Dec. 2010, n. pag. Web. 25 Dec. 2012.

Levine, Robert S. *Martin Delany, Frederick Douglass, and the Politics of Representative Identity*. Chapel Hill: University of North Carolina Press, 1997. Print.

Lewis, Roger. "Money, Love, and Aspiration in *The Great Gatsby*." New Essays on *The Great Gatsby*. Ed. Matthew J. Bruccoli. Cambridge: Cambridge University Press, 1985. 41–57. Print.

Lukács, György. *History and Class Consciousness*. Cambridge: MIT, 1971. Print.

"Lynching in America." *University of Missouri-Kansas City*. Web. 28 Apr. 2010.

Martin, Waldo E. *The Mind of Frederick Douglass*. Chapel Hill: University of North Carolina Press, 1984. Print.

Marvin, Thomas F. *Kurt Vonnegut: A Critical Companion*. Westport: Greenwood, 2002. Print.

Marx, Karl. *Capital: A Critique of Political Economy*. Vol. 1. Trans. Samuel Moore and Edward Aveling. Chicago: Kerr, 1906. Print.

———. *Grundrisse*. Trans. David McLellan. New York: Harper, 1971. Print.

McDowell, Deborah E. "In the First Place: Making Frederick Douglass and the Afro-American Narrative Tradition." *Critical Essays on Frederick Douglass*. Ed. William L. Andrews. Boston: Hall, 1991. 192–214. Print.

McKay, Nellie Y. "Happy[?]-Wife-and-Motherdom: The Portrayal of Ma Joad in John Steinbeck's *The Grapes of Wrath*." *Bloom's Modern Critical Interpretations: John Steinbeck's* The Grapes of Wrath. Ed. Harold Bloom. New York: Chelsea House, 2007, 93–111. Print.

McLellan, David. *Karl Marx: Selected Writings*. Oxford: Oxford University Press, 2000. Print.

Mendenhall, Allen. *Literature and Liberty*. Lanham, MD: Lexington Books, 2014. Print.

Milgrom, Paul, and John Roberts. *Economics, Organization, and Management*. Upper Saddle River: Prentice Hall, 1992. Print.

Miller, James D. *Singularity Rising*. Dallas: BenBella, 2012. Print.

Mises, Ludwig von. *The Anti-Capitalistic Mentality*. 1956. Mansfield Centre: Martino, 2009. Print.

———. *Human Action*. 1949. Auburn: Ludwig von Mises Institute, 2008. Print.

———. *Planning for Freedom: And Sixteen Other Essays and Addresses*. South Holland: Libertarian, 1980. Print.

———. *Socialism: An Economic and Sociological Analysis*. 1951. Auburn: Ludwig von Mises Institute, 2009. Print.

———. *Theory and History: An Interpretation of Social and Economic Evolution*. 1957. Auburn: Ludwig von Mises Institute, 2007. Print.

Morse, Donald E. "We Are Marching to Utopia: Kurt Vonnegut's *Player Piano*. *The Utopian Fantastic*. Ed. Martha Bartter. Westport: Praeger, 2004. 23–32. Print.

Osterfeld, David. "Marxism, Capitalism, and Mercantilism." *The Review of Austrian Economics* 5 (1991): 107–14. Print.

Perloff, Richard. "The Press and Lynchings of African Americans." *Journal of Black Studies* 30 (2000): 315–30. Print.

Posnock, Ross. "'A New World, Material Without Being Real': Fitzgerald's Critique of Capitalism in *The Great Gatsby*." *Critical Essays on Fitzgerald's* The Great Gatsby. Ed. Scott Donaldson. Boston, Hall, 1984. 201–13. Print.

Powell, Jim. *FDR's Folly*. New York: Crown, 2003. Print.

Raico, Ralph. *Classical Liberalism and the Austrian School*. Auburn: Ludwig von Mises Institute, 2012. Print.

"Red Meat and Red Herrings." *Commonweal* 13 Oct. 1939: 562–63. Rpt. in *A Casebook on The Grapes of Wrath*. Ed. Agnes McNeill Donohue. New York: Cromwell, 1968. 71–75. Print.

Reilly, John M., ed. *Richard Wright: The Critical Reception*. New York: Franklin, 1978. Print.

Ricardo, David. *On the Principles of Political Economy and Taxation*. 1817. Ed. E. C. K. Gonner. London: Bell, 1919. Print.

Rifkin, Jeremy. *The End of Work: The Decline of the Global Labor Force and the Dawn of the Post-Market Era*. New York: Putnam, 1995. Print.

Rothbard, Murray. *America's Great Depression*. Auburn: Ludwig von Mises Institute, 2000. Print.

———. "Economic Depressions: Their Causes and Cure." *The Austrian Theory of the Trade Cycle and Other Essays*. Ed. Richard M. Ebeling. Auburn: Ludwig von Mises Institute, 1996. 65–91. Print.

———. *Science, Technology, and Government*. 1959. Auburn: Mises Institute, 2004. Web.

Schultz, Theodore W. *Investing in People*. Berkeley: University of California Press, 1981. Print.

Shulman, Robert. *The Power of Political Art: The 1930's Literary Left Reconsidered*. Chapel Hill: University of North Carolina Press, 2000. Print.

Shakespeare, William. *The Merchant of Venice*. 1600. New York: Simon, 2010. Print.

Smith, Adam. *An Inquiry into the Nature and Causes of the Wealth of Nations*. 1776. New York: Random, 1937. Print.

Sowell, Thomas. *Applied Economics*. New York: Basic, 2009. Print.

———. *Basic Economics*. New York: Basic, 2007. Print.

———. *Black Rednecks and White Liberals*. San Francisco: Encounter, 2005. Print.

———. *Economic Facts and Fallacies*. New York: Basic, 2008. Print.

———. *The Economics and Politics of Race*. New York: Morrow, 1983. Print.

———. *Intellectuals and Society*. New York: Basic, 2009. Print.

———. *Race and Culture*. New York: Basic, 2004. Print.

Standish, David. "*Playboy* Interview." *Conversations with Kurt Vonnegut*. Ed. William Rodney Allen. Jackson: University Press of Mississippi, 1988. 76–110. Print.

Steinbeck, John. *A Life in Letters*. Ed. Elaine Steinbeck and Robert Wallsten. New York: Penguin, 1976. Print.

———. *The Grapes of Wrath*. 1939. New York: Penguin, 1976. Print.

———. *The Harvest Gypsies*. Berkeley: Heyday, 1936. Print.

———. *Working Days: The Journals of The Grapes of Wrath, 1938-1941*. Ed. Robert De-Mott. New York: Viking, 1989. Print.

Stepto, Robert B. "Storytelling in Early Afro-American Fiction: Frederick Douglass's 'The Heroic Slave.'" *Georgia Review* 36 (1982): 355–68. Print.

Stone, Albert E. "Identity and Art in Frederick Douglass's *Narrative*." *CLA Journal* 17 (1973): 192–213. Print.

Sundquist, Eric J. "Frederick Douglass: Literacy and Paternalism." *Raritan* 6.2 (1986): 108–24. Print.

Surowiecki, James. *The Wisdom of Crowds*. New York: Anchor, 2005. Print.

Taylor, Frank J. "California's *Grapes of Wrath*." *Forum* 102 (November 1939): 232–38. Rpt. in *A Casebook on* The Grapes of Wrath. Ed. Agnes McNeill Donohue. New York: Cromwell, 1968. 8–19. Print.

Thernstrom, Stephan, and Abigail Thernstrom. *America in Black and White*. New York: Simon, 1997. Print.

Tratner, Michael. "A Man Is His Bonds: *The Great Gatsby* and Deficit Spending." Ed. Martha Woodmansee and Mark Osteen. *The New Economic Criticism: Studies at the Intersection of Literature and Economics*. New York: Routledge, 1999. 365–77. Print.

Turner, Frederick. *Shakespeare's Twenty-First Century Economics: The Morality of Love and Money*. Oxford: Oxford University Press, 1999. Print.

Veblen, Thornstein. *The Theory of the Leisure Class*. New York: Macmillan, 1899. Print.

Vonnegut, Kurt. *A Man Without A Country*. New York: Seven Stories, 2005. Print.

————. *Player Piano*. 1952. New York: Avon, 1972. Print.

Vonnegut, Kurt, and William R. Allen. *Conversations with Kurt Vonnegut*. Jackson: University Press of Mississippi, 1988. Print.

Wapshott, Nicholas. *Keynes Hayek: The Clash that Defined Modern Economics*. New York: Norton, 2011. Print.

Williams, Raymond. *Marxism and Literature*. Oxford: Oxford University Press, 1977. Print.

Williams, Walter. *The State Against Blacks*. New York: New Press, 1982. Print.

Woodmansee, Martha, and Mark Osteen. *The New Economic Criticism: Studies at the Intersection of Literature and Economics*. New York: Routledge, 1999. Print.

Wright, Richard. *Native Son*. New York: Harper Collins, 1940. Print.

Younkins, Edward. *Capitalism and Commerce in Imaginative Literature: Perspectives on Business from Novels and Plays*. Lanham, MD: Lexington Books, 2016. Print.

Zafar, Rafia. "Franklinian Douglass: The Afro-American as Representative Man." *Frederick Douglass: New Literary and Historical Essays*. Ed. Eric J. Sundquist. Cambridge: Cambridge University Press, 1990. 99–117. Print.

Index

About the Author

Matt Spivey is an English professor and the chair of English and Modern Languages at Arizona Christian University.

Lightning Source UK Ltd.
Milton Keynes UK
UKHW021409111022
410300UK00002B/22